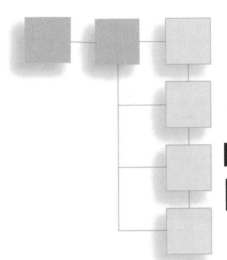

iPhone® Game
Development
for Teens

CLAYTON CROOKS

Course Technology PTR
A part of Cengage Learning

COURSE TECHNOLOGY
CENGAGE Learning·

Australia • Brazil • Japan • Korea • Mexico • Singapore • Spain • United Kingdom • United States

COURSE TECHNOLOGY
CENGAGE Learning·

iPhone® Game Development for Teens
Clayton Crooks

Publisher and General Manager, Course Technology PTR:
Stacy L. Hiquet

Associate Director of Marketing:
Sarah Panella

Manager of Editorial Services:
Heather Talbot

Senior Marketing Manager:
Mark Hughes

Senior Acquisitions Editor: Emi Smith

Project Editor: Jenny Davidson

Technical Reviewer: Michael Duggan

Interior Layout Tech: MPS Limited

Cover Designer: Mike Tanamachi

Indexer: Larry Sweazy

Proofreader: Michael Beady

For product information and technology assistance, contact us at
Cengage Learning Customer & Sales Support, 1-800-354-9706

For permission to use material from this text or product, submit all requests online at **cengage.com/permissions**

Further permissions questions can be emailed to
permissionrequest@cengage.com

Library of Congress Control Number: 2011942310

ISBN-13: 978-1-4354-5992-2

ISBN-10: 1-4354-5992-X

Course Technology, a part of Cengage Learning
20 Channel Center Street
Boston, MA 02210
USA

Cengage Learning is a leading provider of customized learning solutions with office locations around the globe, including Singapore, the United Kingdom, Australia, Mexico, Brazil, and Japan. Locate your local office at: **international.cengage.com/region**

Cengage Learning products are represented in Canada by Nelson Education, Ltd.

For your lifelong learning solutions, visit **courseptr.com**

Visit our corporate website at **cengage.com**

Printed by RR Donnelley. Crawfordsville, IN. 1st Ptg. 03/2012

Printed in the United States of America
1 2 3 4 5 6 7 14 13 12

*This book is affectionately dedicated to my wife, Amy,
and son, Clayton III.*

ACKNOWLEDGMENTS

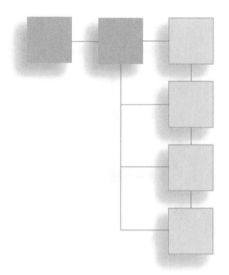

I would like to thank Jenny Davidson and Mike Duggan for putting in the time to review this book for accuracy and for their suggestions to improve it. I would also like to thank everyone at Cengage Learning and, in particular, Emi Smith for her help and patience during the writing of the book. Lastly, I would like to thank Click-team for creating a great set of tools and, specifically, Jeff Vance for his help and suggestions.

ABOUT THE AUTHOR

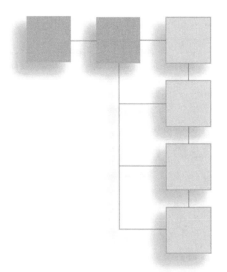

Clayton Crooks is an award-winning author and computer consultant based in Knoxville, TN. Crooks has served as a beta tester for numerous development tools, and he has developed many iOS applications as custom solutions for his clients using the tools discussed in this book. He is a regular contributor to several magazines and websites and has had books published on a range of topics including everything from Visual Basic to game development to 3D graphics.

Contents

INTRODUCTION

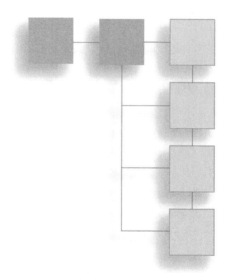

This book provides an introduction to creating games for iOS devices such as the iPhone, iPad, and iPod Touch. It begins with teaching the basics on how to get started in game development and then moves into creating the components for games, such as music, sound effects, and graphics. Once a solid foundation is in place, the book provides step-by-step instructions for building several games.

The book is designed with a complete beginner in mind, and as such, is best read in order. There are a couple of reasons for this. The chapters are organized so that subsequent chapters get progressively more difficult. This way, there is not a sudden jump to a topic that is too difficult for a beginning game developer, and the basic concepts that are learned in each chapter are all combined into several full game projects.

The book was written to teach you game development, so it's only natural that you'd want to know what types of games you create when reading this book. You can skim through the table of contents in the book to see the individual projects that include everything from arcade-style games to card games. Additionally, the book has been designed so that the techniques and concepts you learn can be easily adapted to your own projects to create the games that you would like to build.

COMPANION WEBSITE DOWNLOADS

You may download the companion website files from www.courseptr.com/downloads. Please note that you will be redirected to the Cengage Learning site.

CHAPTER 1

INTRODUCTION TO GAME DEVELOPMENT

Developing games for the iPhone is one of the hottest trends in computing. If you've always wanted to create a game, but didn't know exactly where to start, this book will be your guide through the entire development process. Not only will you learn to create a game, but you will also learn how to draw the graphics for the game, create the sound effects and music, and put it all together into a final project that can be submitted to Apple's App Store. The process can seem a bit daunting, but if you follow the book through from beginning to end, you will have the ability to create games for the iPhone.

However, before you can make a game, there are a number of topics that you will need to understand. We've already mentioned a few, such as the graphics, music, and sound effects, but you will also need to have the proper software and hardware. You can't really make a game without involving most of these elements. Once you have mastered the individual components, you need the ability to put them all together into a final game project.

In this chapter, you will begin your journey into creating games for the iPhone, iPod Touch, and iPad. The book should be followed through chapter by chapter, as each will build upon the previous. This first chapter is like your first day at school; we won't get into too much heavy lifting and will focus on giving you a good foundation that you will continue to build upon until you have created a game of your own.

HISTORY OF GAME DEVELOPMENT

Like any subject, a basic understanding of its history is a good place to begin when you are starting out. If you look on the web or browse through game development magazines, you will find many stories that have been written about small or even one-man development teams. This is very interesting, as the game development industry has undergone some major changes in the last decade. It's actually gone the way of Hollywood movie studios, complete with large budgets into the millions. These large teams and financial backing are making it harder for lone-wolf developers to compete.

At first glance, that seems contradictory to the second sentence of this section. If it were harder to compete, why would there be more small teams that are successful and being acknowledged in the press? The increase in small or single-person development teams can be attributed to some recent changes in the market that has allowed thousands of amateur developers to create profitable and exciting games. In fact, we could argue that the game development industry is undergoing one of its biggest changes in its short history, and the success of small and one-man shops is directly related to something that is behind some of the upheaval.

You might be wondering what has happened that has changed the world of game development so dramatically. It isn't a set of tools, or even a particular set of new development applications. Rather, it is the proliferation of games for mobile devices, smart phones, and specifically, the iPhone. That's why we're going to focus on the iPhone in this book, but it's worth noting that the processes you learn in the construction of your iPhone game will serve as an excellent base and would be useful if you decide to develop for the Mac, PC, web, or other mobile operating systems such as Android.

You can compete with the bigger players in game development, but ideally, you won't have to directly compete. You can focus on a particular niche area of games such as platform games or sports games. Additionally, with the Apple App Store being available to sell, you have the same number of people looking at your offerings as even the largest development company. It's this change in marketing, and the advent of cheaper and smaller hardware that makes it possible for you to enjoy success as a one-man shop. As of the time of writing, more than 15 billion downloads have occurred in the Apple App Store. That's a staggering figure, and you can quickly see how you can carve out a nice niche in such a large number of purchases.

Note

Anytime you see "App Store" in the book, it is referring to Apple's App Store.

SETTING UP A SMALL GAME STUDIO

Before we can actually get started in making any games, we need to make sure we have the proper tools at our disposal. This doesn't mean breaking the bank, as setting up a small game development studio doesn't have to be all that expensive. There are ways you can save money when getting started. For example, when looking at various types of software, there are some open source and free options that will do some of the same functions as their commercial counterparts. With Moore's Law (this basically predicts that the processing power of computers will double every 18 months) continuing to hold true, the cost of computers continues to plummet. There are great deals for relatively powerful computers everywhere you look. Fortunately, you may already have the essentials of a game studio—a computer and this book; however, we will look closer at how to determine if what you have is enough and the best way to determine what more you may need.

Note

> What is open source? Rather than a commercial license where a company is paid for the work and their product is protected by copyright, open-source products have program code openly shared and maintained by hundreds or even thousands of developers with the goal of creating something that can be given away for free.

For this book, and iPhone development in general, you'll need to have access to an Intel-based Mac OS computer to compile your final project. OS stands for Operating System and it is the software that controls a computer's basic functions like executing applications and controlling peripherals. If you decide to purchase a Mac, make sure it's an Intel-based system as the older PowerPC options will not work. Apple's Software Developers Kit (SDK) is only available on Intel-based Macs, and although many tools exist for the creation of iPhone OS apps and games on Windows, you will need a Mac to compile the final output. This is also true for the tools we'll use in the book. The applications we'll be using for the graphics and development are Windows-based, so if you already have a Windows PC, you can do everything in the book with the exception of compiling to the iOS (Apple's mobile operating system that runs on iPhone, iPod Touch, and iPad). You can create all of the projects, and even do basic testing, but you will need to find a friend with a Mac, or locate someone on a freelance site that will do it for a fee. This will only be needed to do the final compile so that your project can be submitted to the App Store.

If you are purchasing a new computer for iOS game development, consider buying a Mac. This is the best option as you can then also choose to run Windows in a number of ways on your Mac by using special software applications, some of which are freely available. The options include Apple's Boot Camp, Parallels, VMWare, or Virtual Box. I'll leave it up to you to decide the best option for you, but all of them are more than adequate. Your computer can be a notebook or a desktop, depending on your other intended uses.

Note

I'll keep a list of links to the tools and software that are used in this book at my website www.claytoncrooks.com.

Software and Other Equipment

The next item, and one that is often overlooked by beginners as well as experienced developers, is a method of backing up everything that you create. Be careful, because although you may have a new PC, a single hard drive crash, virus, or spyware can bring an entire project to a quick and painful ending. There are a number of ways to back up your software and graphics including DVD/CD burners, external hard drives, USB memory sticks, and online backup options to name a few. Each would be more than sufficient to back up your projects. Choose one, or if you are particularly concerned, even more than one to make sure you have good backups. Nothing stops a project quicker than an unforeseen computer disaster.

Another interesting item that could come in handy is a Digitizer, which is something that an artist will use. If you are a one-man development team, you wear all the hats, which includes being the artist. Digitizers are pen-like devices that allow you to draw more naturally into the computer. This is far from a necessity, and can be expensive, but if your budget allows, the time you will save will be tremendous. The less expensive digital pens have fewer options, but if you have a tight budget, even the least expensive digitizer would come in handy.

A scanner is something that an artist can use as well. It allows you to draw your items on paper and then convert them into a digital format that your computer can use. A multi-function machine with a printer and scanner can be had for a relatively small amount of money. Again, you don't necessarily need one, but a scanner and a printer can make your graphics life much easier.

One important item to not forget is a surge-protector, which will help protect your PC and peripherals from power surges that occur through your electrical outlets. These surges happen regularly, and for a small fee, you have an added level of protection. There are other options for surge protection that offer additional safety and will be discussed later.

We'll cover specific software later in the chapter. At this time, you should know that you would need several different types of software to create a game:

1. Graphics applications for drawing and creating designs

2. Development software for creating the game

3. Music and sound effects

Network and Internet Access

Having access to the Internet is a must for iOS development, and having a network is another item that can be very helpful. If you have more than one computer, it will allow your computers to communicate with each other. For example, if you have a Mac desktop to compile your final apps and a Windows notebook for creating the components, you can network them together and easily transfer files between them. While this sounds like a complex and expensive undertaking, it is a very easily achievable goal and inexpensive with today's technology.

Along with file sharing, there are a few additional benefits of a home network, such as shared peripherals and resources. You can have one scanner, printer, or device on the network that other computers can access. We've already mentioned the importance of backing up, and you can use a network to back up data on multiple PCs easily. With the advent of cheap wireless routers, a wireless network is a fantastic option for you to investigate.

You'll definitely need some type of Internet access to upload your projects and to download things that you'll need. One final thing you should check into is often overlooked but very important: a good desk and chair. You will be sitting for long periods of time and this will prove to be an invaluable investment.

Tips for Buying Equipment

Now that you have some ideas about the type of hardware you'll need to purchase, there are a few common sense ideas to keep in mind:

- **Use a Credit Card.** You should use a credit card every time you buy something online. If you don't have a credit card, you can have a parent or a friend do this for you. You will need to make sure you have the permission of your parent if you are wishing to use their credit card, and it would be wise to have them help you with your purchases. If you use a credit card, you have the credit card company to back you up in case of a dispute of a purchase. For example, if you receive a broken computer from a purchase, you have the ability to make a dispute to get the charges reversed or the situation remedied.

- **Spend on Important Things.** You should avoid the "budget" computers most of the time and look for something a little higher. These budget systems may not be any cheaper when you factor in that they may not include all of the components that you need such as memory or a large hard drive. Warranties are simply guarantees that an item will be repaired or replaced if the purchaser has a problem in a given period of time. For example, most computers have one-year warranties when purchased, and during that period of time, if something were to happen such as a hard drive crashing, the manufacturer would replace the hard drive at no cost to the purchaser. Extended warranties can be tricky and expensive as they are often times not issued by the original manufacturer but instead by a third party like a store or insurance company. Make sure to check what the warranty will and will not cover, and depending on your experience with computers, it may be a good idea. Most new systems have warranties for the first year but they usually only cover manufacturing defects.

- **Protect Everything.** This will be my final mention of this, but please try to back up your data daily as you can never be too safe. If you have the money, you should purchase a battery-supported surge protector or UPS (Uninterruptible Power Source). For around $50–$100 you can get one that will protect several components. In addition to the added protection, a UPS will allow you plenty of time to save your work and shut down your computer if the power goes out. Surge protectors are easy to use, but they are not completely foolproof.

- **Research.** Above everything that is mentioned, the best thing you can do is spend some time reading and learning about computers for yourself. It's important to make an educated decision on your purchases.

- **Try It Out.** If possible, head to a local store and look at various computer configurations. See how a 15" notebook looks and feels when compared to a 17" notebook. Maybe you will find that the larger screen is better, or that you like the smaller screen and easier portability. Remember that buying a computer is a personal decision that is impacted by so many different variables. The type of computer that one person uses on a daily basis is not necessarily the best purchase for you. Lastly, as you ask for advice from others, it's important to remember that most people are very biased about their own systems, so be careful when opinion-hunting for computer systems among individuals.

ACQUIRING THE SOFTWARE

Earlier in the chapter, we briefly mentioned the types of software you are going to need. For a single-person development team, you will definitely need software for creating the graphic elements for your game. These graphic elements include the obvious items that you see on the screen such as a spaceship or an asteroid, but they may also include the design of a Graphical User Interface (GUI—pronounced "gooey"). We will begin our search for graphics software, and will also lightly cover the basic information for the other applications we'll need.

The GIMP

The GIMP, short for GNU Image Manipulation Program, can be seen in Figure 1.1. It is a freely distributed program that can be used for a wide range of tasks, including photo retouching, image composition, and image authoring. It has many capabilities that rival those of the industry-leading Adobe Photoshop, but it lacks one important element: its high price. For our purposes, it will be used as a paint program for designing and creating graphics elements for our game.

GIMP is available at www.gimp.com, where you should download the most recent version for your operating system. GIMP is written and developed under X11 on

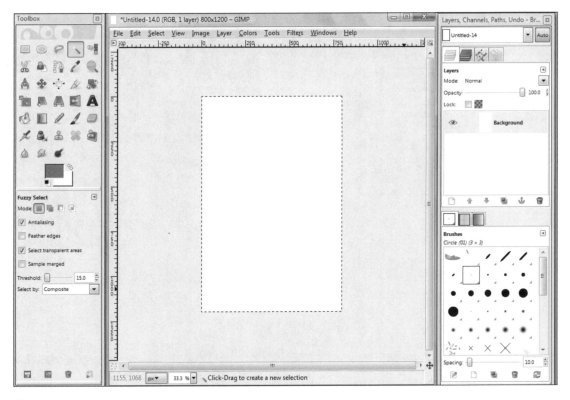

Figure 1.1
The GIMP has a nice interface that is easy to use.

UNIX platforms, but is available for MS Windows and Mac OS X as well. Figures in this book that include the GIMP will refer to the interface of the Windows version, but for the most part, every version is the same.

Once you download the GIMP for your OS, you can move to the optional next step, downloading the iOS SDK.

iOS SDK

Another piece of software that you will need to download is the iOS SDK, a component of which can be seen in Figure 1.2, if you have a Mac. If not, you can skip over this section and let someone compile your code into its final version for you. It is freely available from Apple's iOS Developers Center (http://developer.apple.com). It's a huge download, so make some time for this to finish. Even on a high-speed connection, it may take a few hours. The installation is straightforward and relatively painless. If you decide to put your game on your own device for testing, or if you wish to put it on the App Store, you will need to join the iOS Developer Program,

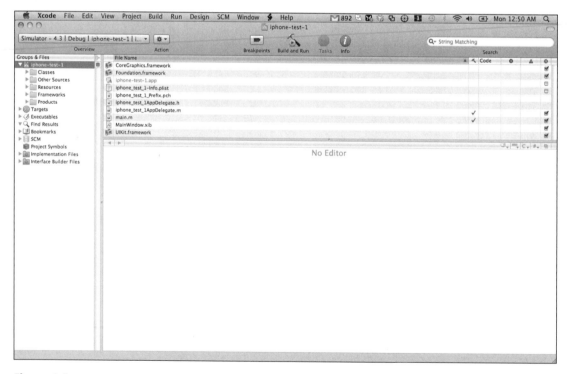

Figure 1.2
The iOS SDK.

which is priced at $99/year at the time of writing. You do not need to join to download the SDK, so at this time, even if you are planning to do so later, you should not spend the money on the developer program. Wait until you have finished the book, and are ready to create your own games, before spending this money. Because it is a yearly fee, this will help you save some time rather than having weeks or months slip away from your subscription while you are learning.

Multimedia Fusion

Our game development tool of choice for this book is Multimedia Fusion (Figure 1.3), a fantastic tool that can be used for creating games and applications for Windows, Mac, Android, Flash, Microsoft XNA, and iOS. Multimedia Fusion, or MMF as it is commonly referred to, is a tool that runs on Windows, and at the time of writing, many of the exporters, which allow for the programs to run on various platforms, are in

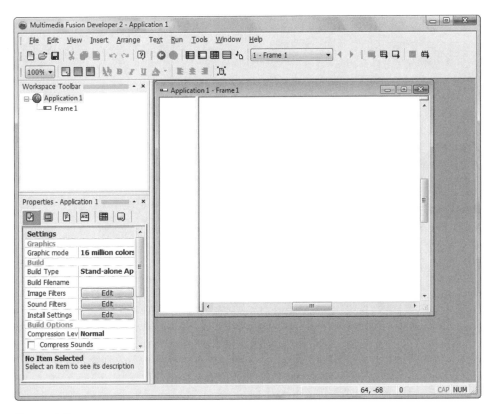

Figure 1.3
Multimedia Fusion running in Windows.

Beta and may or may not be available in final version when the book is printed. For the most up-to-date information, you can check out my website (www.claytoncrooks.com). Once there, please check my links under the book to download the newest Multimedia Fusion available. We'll cover the installation process of Multimedia Fusion in Chapter 4.

Sound and Music Software

We need some software for creating music as well as sound effects for our game, as it probably wouldn't be too much fun to play a game without sound. We're going to use Audacity, an open-source sound editor, for creating and editing sound effects. It can be seen in Figure 1.4. To create the music, we'll use a piece of software called Sony ACID Xpress that utilizes loops to create all types of music. An example of Sony ACID Xpress can be seen in Figure 1.5.

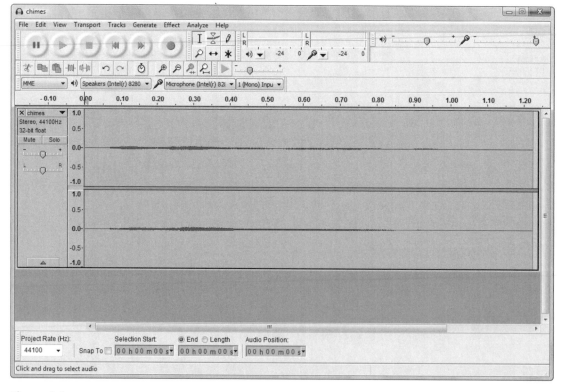

Figure 1.4
Audacity is a free sound editor.

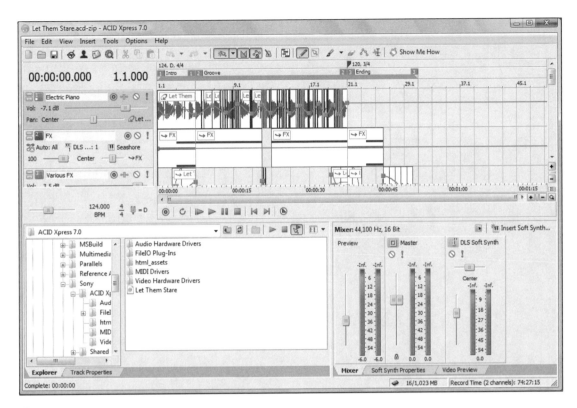

Figure 1.5
A loop-based music editor called ACID Xpress.

CHAPTER REVIEW

In this chapter, we looked at the basic components that you will need to create your own game development studio. Once you have assembled your game development studio and have your PC up and running, whether it is an off-the-shelf special or the latest and greatest system money can buy, you will have made a huge step toward becoming a game developer. The next step is to learn the basic building blocks of a game.

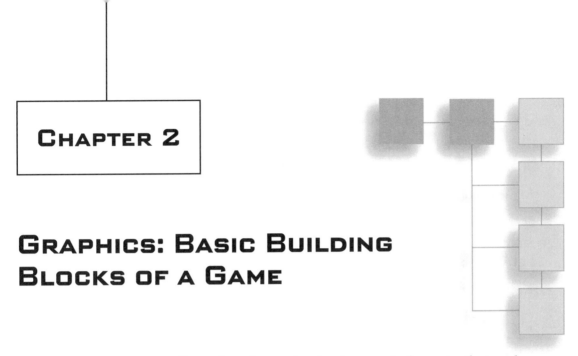

CHAPTER 2

GRAPHICS: BASIC BUILDING BLOCKS OF A GAME

To create games, you will need to learn the fundamental elements that make up a game. These elements are each necessary and include graphics and sounds (music and sound effects). Although the ability to interact with a device to play a game is important, the basics of interactivity change depending on the type of game and device you are using. With that in mind, we will concern ourselves with the core building blocks that exist in nearly every game.

We'll use this basic approach to help you break down and understand a game in your mind at its most fundamental level. Because this is the core of graphic design, this knowledge can be used in many areas beyond game development and can be applied in a variety of areas in computers.

GRAPHICS

When we talk about sights in a game, we are talking about what you see on the screen during gameplay. In any major production, from a website to a game, the layout of the screens and the graphic images that are used to make them are very important. In a larger development team, they are usually worked on by a number of people including a designer, producer, art director, and others. In a one-person development effort, you will need to wear several hats and try to perform the actions of all of them.

The creation of the assets that will be used in the making of the interface elements can require the use of many software tools and techniques. The assets are often sketched on paper or mocked up on the computer before they are created. Some of the tools used are 2D paint programs like the GIMP that work only with flat images, 3D programs that allow you to build and render objects that realistically recreate a 3D environment or object, and even digital photos and scans are used. In order to create the images, you will need to have an understanding of the concepts of the images and a grasp on the tools you will be using.

2D art assets include, but are not limited to, the following:

- **Menus.** Look at the menu screens in your favorite games, and specifically in some iPhone games to see an example of the layouts.

- **Credits.** These screens often contain logos and information related to those that have worked on a game project.

- **User Interface.** These are background images, buttons, cursors, and other art objects a user can click on or interact with. This is especially important for iPhone games that use fingers for input.

- **Graphics.** When you play a game, the graphics you encounter such as the characters in a game and the surrounding environments.

In computer graphics there are two basic types of art: 3-Dimensional (3D) and 2-Dimensional (2D). 2D images are a flat image with no depth while 3D art shows depth, as illustrated in Figure 2.1.

The three dimensions are described in X, Y, and Z coordinates in a system known as the Cartesian coordinate system. X is a horizontal line (or axis), Y is a vertical line, and Z is the distance backward and forward (see Figures 2.2, 2.3, and 2.4). This

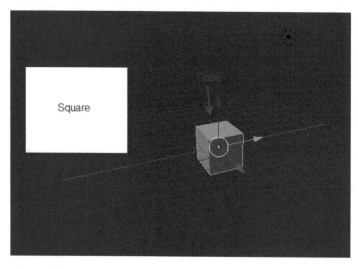

Figure 2.1
A square is 2D whereas a cube is 3D.

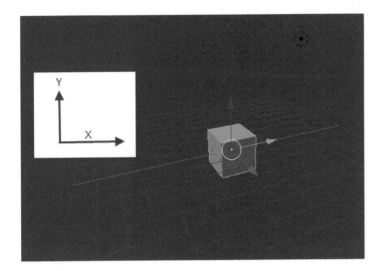

Figure 2.2
The Cartesian coordinate system.

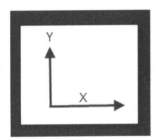

Figure 2.3
A square with X and Y values.

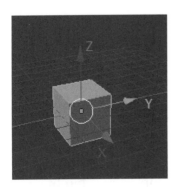

Figure 2.4
Cube with X, Y, and Z.

Figure 2.5
The stick figure is made up of pixels, the smallest unit of a computer image.

might sound familiar to you depending on how much math you have already been introduced to. For a young developer, it's actually quite exciting to discover that you can actually use some of that math you've been studying at school. In fact, algebra, geometry, and physics all play a role in game making.

Basic Elements of an Image

To properly understand 2D images, you must learn about their basic elements, beginning with the smallest component, a picture element, commonly referred to as a pixel. A *pixel* is simply a colored dot on a screen. Every computer image, television image, or image on your iPhone is made up of these pixels that are arranged in rows and columns. (See Figure 2.5 for an illustration of a pixel.) No matter how big and fancy a computer image is, if it's a black-and-white image of a square box or a photograph with millions of colors, it is all just a bunch of pixels arranged in rows and columns.

It's important to understand that once an image is created in the computer, or scanned or otherwise transferred into a computer, the maximum detail is already set and cannot be increased. You can increase or decrease the size of an image in the computer, but this resizing is actually done by a mathematical process called interpolation. Take a look at Figures 2.6 and 2.7. The same stick figure we looked at in Figure 2.5 is enlarged and then shrunken. You can see this process does not increase the detail, but instead, the software uses interpolation to add extra pixels between areas to smooth the transition between the original pixels.

Resolution

Resolution is a number calculated by taking the width of the pixels and multiplying that number by the number of pixels of height. This number is represented in dots per inch (DPI). An image that is to be printed usually needs to be a minimum of

Figure 2.6
The same figure enlarged.

Figure 2.7
Here is the same figure shrunken.

300 dpi (dots per inch). You will often see screen resolutions of 320 × 200, 640 × 480, 800 × 600, 1024 × 768, 1152 × 864, and 1280 × 1024. For example, an 800 × 600 resolution means that your screen will be 800 pixels wide (horizontal) and 600 pixels high (vertical). (See the examples in Figures 2.8, 2.9, and 2.10.)

Aspect Ratio

Another important component of resolution is *aspect ratio*. This is a calculation based on the ratio of the pixel's width to the pixel's height, and it's important because not all images are perfectly square. This is easiest to see by example, so take a look at Figures 2.11 and 2.12. They show a circular figure that is originally created in 320 × 200 and then displayed in 640 × 480. You will notice that the image appears slightly flattened and egg shaped, since the pixels are more narrow.

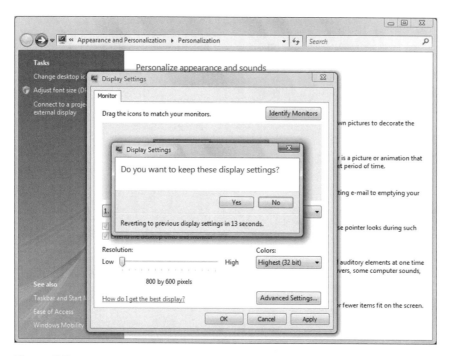

Figure 2.8
Here is the Windows Desktop at 800 × 600 dots per inch.

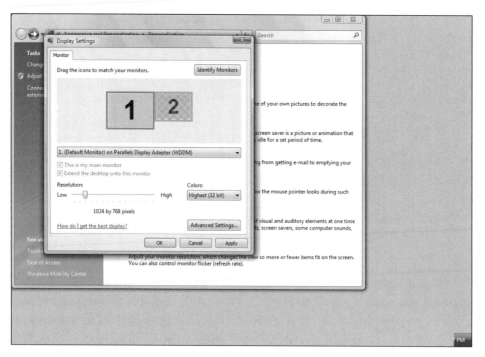

Figure 2.9
Here is the Windows Desktop at 1024 × 768 dots per inch.

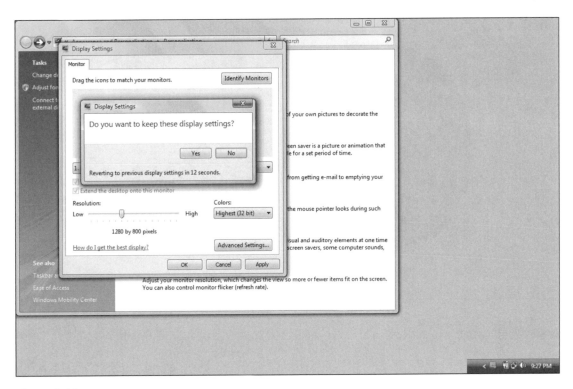

Figure 2.10
Here is the Windows Desktop at 1280 × 800 dots per inch.

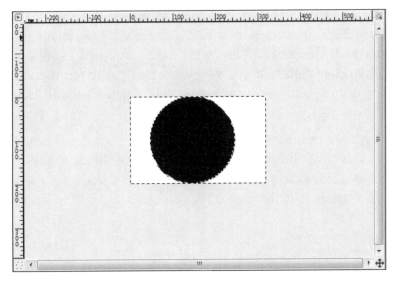

Figure 2.11
Here is an image created at 320 × 200 dots per inch.

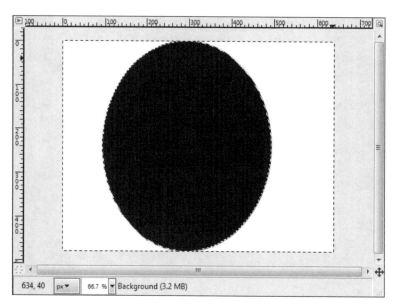

Figure 2.12
Here is the same image displayed in 640 × 480 mode.

Colors

The next topic that you need to understand is color, and specifically how color works in a computer. In games, you often have to set precise color information to achieve a desired goal. This is where an RGB value comes into the picture. RGB is a calculation that is a mixture of the colors Red, Green, and Blue, which are combined in various amounts to make up all of the other colors. If you've ever mixed paint together, or created a green color by mixing blue and yellow crayons, you will understand how this works.

RGB values are represented by three numbers each separated by a comma. For example, an RGB of 0,0,255 means you have all Blue and no Red or Green. Black would be 0,0,0 and white would be 255,255,255. RGB graphics can include up to, but not more than, 256 colors (0 to 255). In Figures 2.13 through 2.17, you can see the RGB values of various common colors.

Note

You may also hear color referred to as CMYK, which is a mode used by traditional printing processes and stands for Cyan, Magenta, Yellow, and Black. You will probably never use CMYK color in game creation; instead, you will deal with the aforementioned RGB or indexed color.

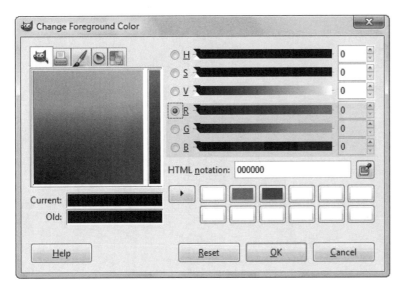

Figure 2.13
This is the RGB color palette for black.

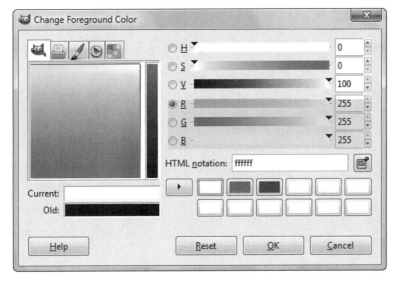

Figure 2.14
This is the RGB color palette for white.

Color Variations

A computer video card can display a certain number of colors at a time, varying from a few, such as 16 colors, up to millions of colors. Because they are in black-and-white in the book, you may have difficulty seeing the differences in Figures 2.18, 2.19, 2.20, and 2.21, representing the same image displayed using increasing numbers of colors.

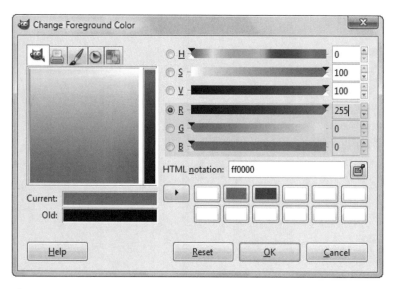

Figure 2.15
This is the RGB color palette for red.

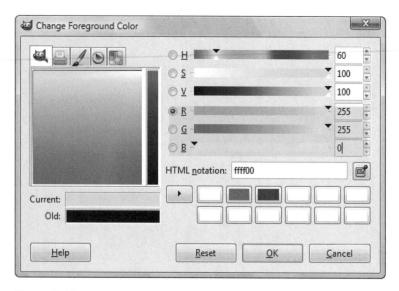

Figure 2.16
This is the RGB color palette for yellow.

This number of colors is referred to as *color depth*, which is simply a description of how many colors can be displayed on your screen at a single time. Color depth is described in terms of bits, and refers to the amount of memory used to represent a single pixel. The most common values are 8-bit, 16-bit, 24-bit, and 32-bit color. More bits correspond to a wider range of colors that can be displayed at a time.

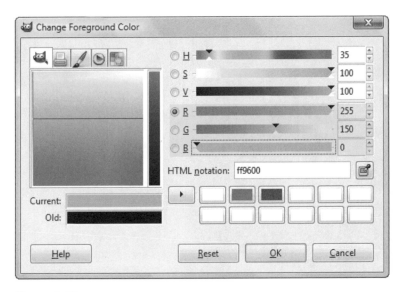

Figure 2.17
This is the RGB color palette for orange.

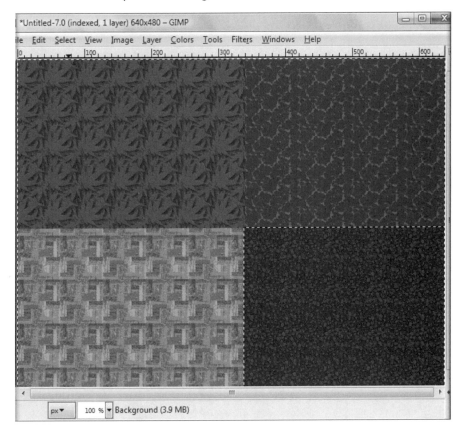

Figure 2.18
This is an image in 16 colors.

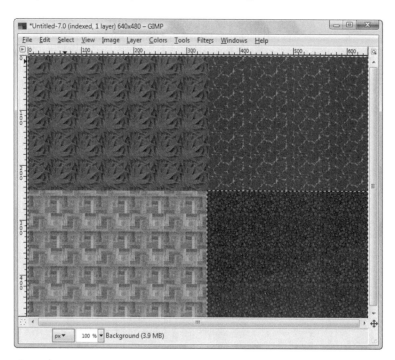

Figure 2.19
This is an image in 256 colors.

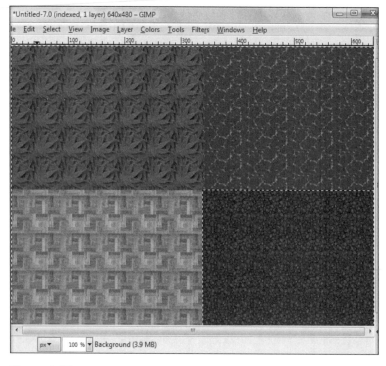

Figure 2.20
This is an image in thousands of colors.

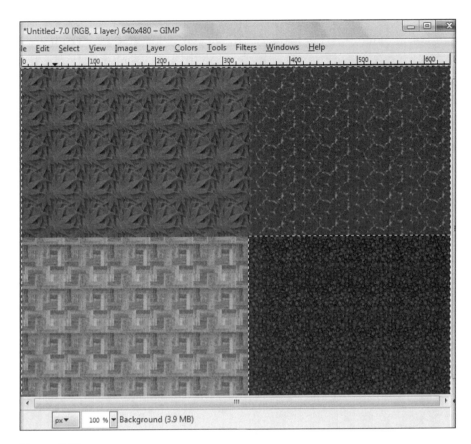

Figure 2.21
This is an image in millions of colors.

Color depths are very interesting. If you were to use True-Color, or 24-bit color, it is capable of displaying 16.8 million colors for every pixel that is on the screen at the same time. However, a human eye cannot distinguish the difference between so many different colors. High-Color is the next lower option, which can display 32,000 or 64,000 colors followed up by 256-Color, which is the most limited. 256-Color stores its color in a palette, and each palette can be set to any of thousands or millions of different color values, but the screen won't show more than 256 different colors at a single time. Some games still use these because, like resolution, more colors means more data pumped to the screen. So if you can get away with only 256 colors, you can render (or draw) the game pictures to the screen faster.

Note

The word render is often used in games, and especially in real-time 3D games, as the computer and software literally render or build an image as they need it. In a 3D game, you can control how each frame looks by where you go in the world and by what you do. This is different from a movie where someone pre-creates the frames in a specific sequence that you cannot change.

You've already seen that a pixel can have a numerical value from 0 to 255. You can see an example of a color palette in Figure 2.22. If you wish to change a color in a 256-color image, you simply replace the color in the palette and it will be changed in the image. You can see an example of this in Figures 2.23 and 2.24.

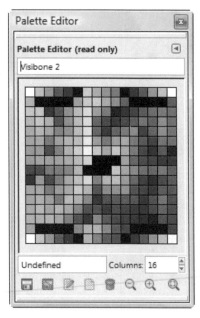

Figure 2.22
You can only see shades of gray here, but the squares are 256 colors.

Figure 2.23
This is a 256-color image.

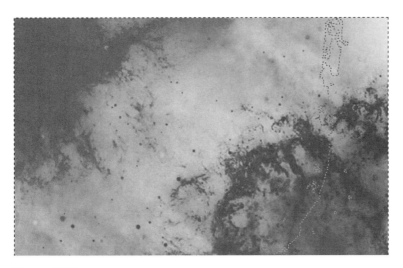

Figure 2.24
This is the same image after changing the palette colors.

CHAPTER REVIEW

This chapter is a good introduction to the various elements that make up and affect images on the computer. This chapter didn't show any work inside of the GIMP, but it was necessary so that you understand image basics. The next chapter will turn to manipulating images.

CHAPTER 3

MANIPULATING IMAGES AND THE GIMP

During the development of your project, you will have to manipulate images in order to get them to fit your needs and design. In this chapter, we're going to look at some of the basics of image manipulation followed by an introduction to tools included in the GIMP that will help you to create your game graphics. Some of the basics of image manipulation are similar to the text editing that you may have done in a word processor with commands such as Cut, Copy, and Paste. If you have never used a word processor or these commands, don't worry; they will be explained fully. Many more commands such as Skew, Rotate, Resize, Crop, and Flip are commonly used.

- **Cut.** If you cut an image, you remove it from the scene. You can paste it back in or undo your action if you make a mistake.

- **Copy.** Copy does not alter your image, but it creates a copy in the memory of your computer. You can paste it in somewhere else, as shown in Figure 3.1.

- **Paste.** As mentioned above, after cutting or copying an image, you can paste it into a different file or somewhere else in the same image, as shown in Figure 3.2, which shows a section cut and pasted.

- **Skew.** You can use skew to slant, deform, or distort an image, as shown in Figure 3.3.

- **Rotate.** Rotating is pretty self-explanatory and can be seen in Figure 3.4.

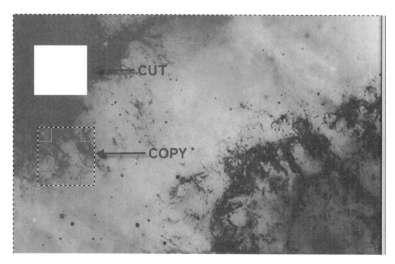

Figure 3.1
Copying and cutting part of an image.

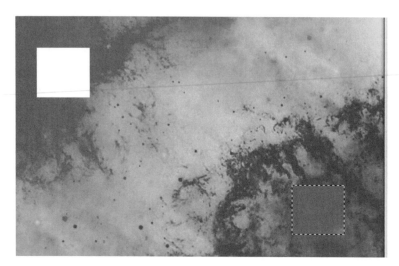

Figure 3.2
Pasting a small section of the image.

- **Resize.** Resizing an image is useful, but as we mentioned in Chapter 2, resizing the image is actually a mathematical calculation that can degrade the image, something that is illustrated in Figures 3.5, 3.6, and 3.7.

- **Crop.** Cropping actually cuts an image to a defined area, as shown in Figures 3.8 and 3.9.

- **Flip.** You can flip images horizontally and vertically. (See Figures 3.10, 3.11, and 3.12.)

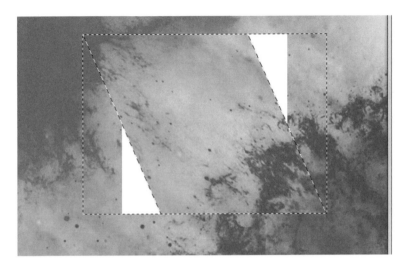

Figure 3.3
Skewing a section of an image.

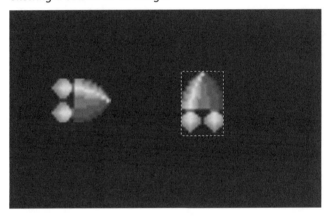

Figure 3.4
Rotating an image of a spaceship 90 degrees.

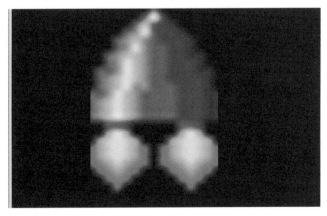

Figure 3.5
Spaceship image blown up.

Figure 3.6
An image reduced.

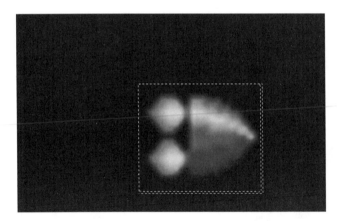

Figure 3.7
The image enlarged to its original size.

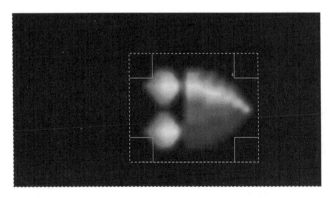

Figure 3.8
The spaceship image selection.

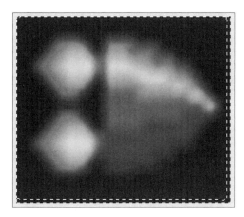

Figure 3.9
The image was cropped and everything outside the crop outline is removed.

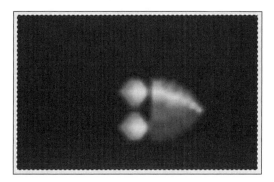

Figure 3.10
The original image before flipping.

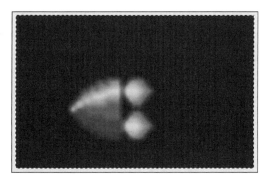

Figure 3.11
The image flipped horizontally.

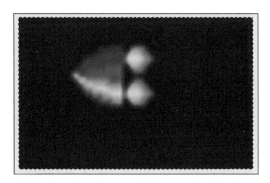

Figure 3.12
The image flipped vertically.

Note

The options for cutting, copying, pasting, skewing, rotating, resizing, cropping, and flipping are all available in the GIMP. We will actually go through the processes as needed when we create our graphics, but for now, you need to simply follow along without worrying about doing any of these actions.

SPRITES AND ANIMATION

Sprites are small pictures of items that move around on the screen in a game, such as characters moving across a platform or objects that you can shoot. Sprites can be a single graphic image or they can be animated. An example of a sprite is shown in Figure 3.13, and the same sprite can be seen placed on a larger background image as shown in Figure 3.14.

Sprite animation is done just like cartoon animation. If you have ever drawn a flip-book to try to make a stick figure walk, you already have an understanding of how this works. A series of images is played in sequence to make it appear that something is moving, such as an explosion or a spinning spaceship. Examples of sprite frames can be seen in Figures 3.15 and 3.16.

Figure 3.13
A sprite image.

Figure 3.14
A sprite in a game.

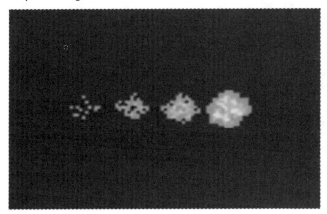

Figure 3.15
A series of sprite images for a game animation.

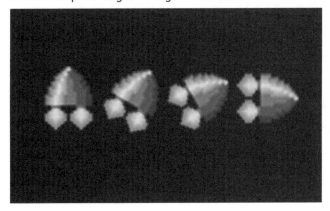

Figure 3.16
A series of sprite images for a rotating ship.

ADVANCED MANIPULATION

Along with the basic tools we have already looked at, we will begin to introduce some more advanced image manipulation techniques. Let's start with a mask, which works kind of like a stencil and allows the edges of your sprites to be any shape and the game will render the masked portions invisible (see Figures 3.17, 3.18, and 3.19).

Color Masking

Another way masking can be achieved is by using a specific color that will ultimately be rendered as clear or transparent, and thus invisible to your user. This color is

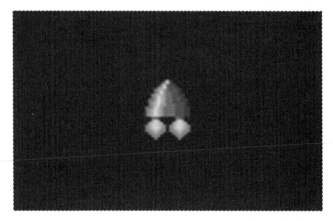

Figure 3.17
An image of a ship.

Figure 3.18
The mask for the ship image.

Figure 3.19
The mask and image combined in a scene.

usually a green shade that will likely not be used at any other time in the game. If you were to use the exact same color for the mask and another area, both would be rendered transparent, so be careful to choose masks that are definitely not used anywhere else.

Palette or Positional Masking

Some games use a specific position on a color palette to determine what color will not render or render transparently. Usually the last color location on the palette is used, so instead of rendering a certain color, it will render whatever color is in the designated position of the color palette as clear.

Opacity

Images can also be displayed in games as opaque, which is simply an image that is halfway between solid and clear. You can think of something like water or a window. Opacity is achieved by looking at the pixels in the image and the pixel directly under it. You can then create a new pixel that is a blended value of the original pixels (see Figures 3.20 and 3.21).

Anti-Aliasing

Look really carefully at the images in Figures 3.22, 3.23, and 3.24, and you will notice that there are very jagged edges on the letters. Those edges are actually just pixels, which is something we have been discussing for some time now. The letters look

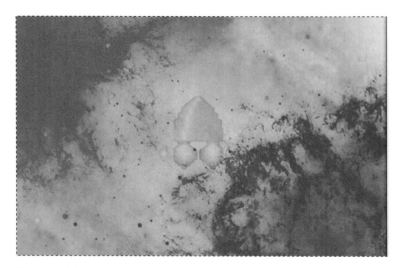

Figure 3.20
The masked ship with opacity set at 25%.

Figure 3.21
A close-up detail of the ship.

Figure 3.22
This image has no anti-aliasing.

Figure 3.23
This image has anti-aliasing.

Figure 3.24
Here is a close-up of both of the image's edges.

particularly jagged if made from a solid color, but by using various shades of a color, and gradually blending the edge color with the background color, it will make the transition smooth and will fool the eye from a distance. This technique is called *anti-aliasing.* It is the reason why images composed of more colors look better than images comprised of fewer colors. Larger number of colors blend more gradually.

GRAPHIC FORMATS

Graphic images are stored in many file formats that are usually best suited to a single type of use. Some image formats are quite large since they retain a lot of image data, whereas some formats are greatly compressed and strip out data for a smaller file

Figure 3.25
This 640 × 480 image is in the BMP format. It is 3.8MB.

Figure 3.26
This 640 × 480 image is a compressed JPEG and is only 80K.

size. Still other formats degrade the image so the file size can be even smaller. This is particularly useful for graphics that are created for mobile games. You will see in Figures 3.25 and 3.26 two versions of an image that are saved in various formats. The degradation is there (see Figure 3.27), but considering the file size of the first image is almost 50 times the size of the JPEG image, it is a trade-off that is more than worthwhile.

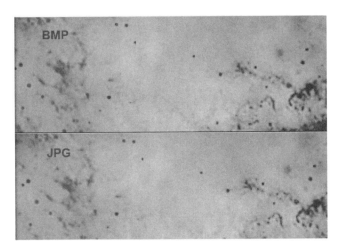

Figure 3.27
Here is a close-up of the same area of both images.

INTRODUCTION TO THE GIMP

GIMP is an excellent graphics editor and is a great choice for game developers. Currently at version 2.6, GIMP offers a tremendous number of features and is a completely free product. It supports a wide range of graphics formats. For game designs and texture creation, GIMP offers everything you need in one easy-to-use package.

If you've followed along from the first chapter, you will have already downloaded and installed the GIMP. If you have not done so, please do so now as we are going to begin working with it. Double-click the shortcut GIMP on your desktop or in the Start menu. When it first starts, a window will be displayed that looks like Figure 3.28.

GUI

The GIMP's GUI (Graphical User Interface, pronounced "gooey") is a very good design for a user interface as it provides excellent functionality but is very easy to learn. Figure 3.29 includes labels for all of the user interface elements. In the next step, we'll look at several of the labeled entries in more detail.

The Toolbar

The GIMP Toolbar contains options for performing many routine tasks like opening, closing, saving, and copying or pasting. The toolbar displays buttons corresponding to the menu commands. It's much easier to click the toolbar button instead of looking through the menu for the corresponding option. If a command is available, you can click on it. Otherwise, it will appear to be "grayed out" and will be unavailable for selection.

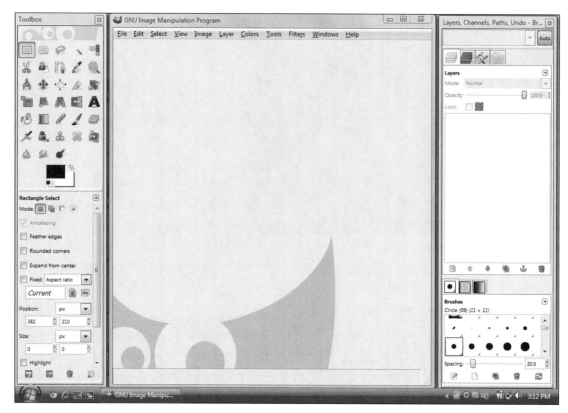

Figure 3.28
The GIMP user interface.

Toolbox

The Toolbox contains the painting, drawing, and retouching tools. You can see the tools in Figure 3.30.

Tool Options Dialog

When you click a Toolbox button, the Tool Options dialog, which is displayed directly beneath the Toolbox, displays the options associated with the tool. You will see the options for the Pencil tool in Figure 3.31.

Layers, Channels, Paths Dialog

The Layers, Channels, Paths dialog, seen in Figure 3.32, is displayed on the right-hand side of the screen and shows the layer structure of the currently active image, and allows you to manipulate the layers in a variety of ways. It is possible to do some basic graphics and editing without taking advantage of the Layers dialog, but if you take the time to learn layers, it will be a huge benefit.

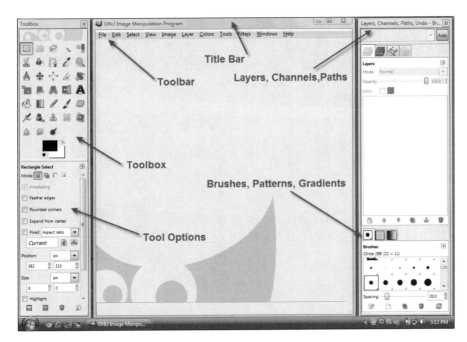

Figure 3.29
The GIMP interface with everything labeled.

Figure 3.30
The Toolbox is important and has a variety of drawing, painting, and retouching tools.

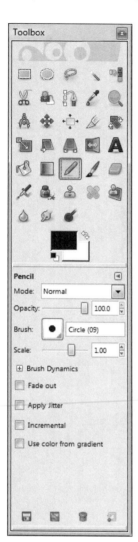

Figure 3.31
The Tool Options for a Pencil.

Brushes/Patterns/Gradients   This docked dialog below the Layers dialog shows the options for managing brushes, patterns, and gradients so that, for example, you can paint with a solid color, a texture, or a gradient.

Painting Tools

GIMP provides several tools that you can use for painting. You will use these tools on a regular basis so we'll take some time to learn the most important features.

Figure 3.32
Manipulating layers in the GIMP is very easy.

Paintbrush Tool

The Paintbrush is useful for painting freehand, much like you would with a regular paintbrush. You simply select the Paintbrush tool and click and drag the cursor while holding a mouse button. If you want to apply the current foreground color, hold down the left mouse button and releasing the button ends your current painting. If you would like to create straight lines, you should hold down the Shift key and click the beginning point. Then, move to where you would like the line to end and click again. Figure 3.33 displays the differences between freehand drawing and holding down the Shift key to draw straight lines.

Eraser

You can use the Eraser to remove pixels from an image, replacing them with the currently selected background color. You can easily restore a mistake by pressing Ctrl-Z (on a Mac Cmd + Z) or selecting Undo from the Edit menu.

Airbrush Tool

The Airbrush tool works in much the same way as the standard Paintbrush tool but instead of a solid color, it simulates an airbrush or spray can. You can use it to draw

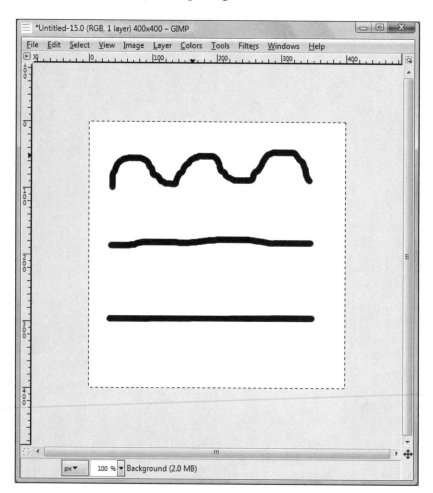

Figure 3.33
Painting freehand or making straight lines with the Paintbrush.

freehand or by holding the Shift key, you can force it to draw straight lines. Figure 3.34 displays a sample of painting comparing the standard Paintbrush and the Airbrush.

Brushes

GIMP's brushes (some of the built-in brushes are shown in Figure 3.35) allow you to paint with a variety of pre-existing shapes or objects. You can add everything from raindrops to flowers to an image very quickly. There are hundreds of brushes on the Internet, or you can use the ones that come with the program. You can even design your own with GIMP.

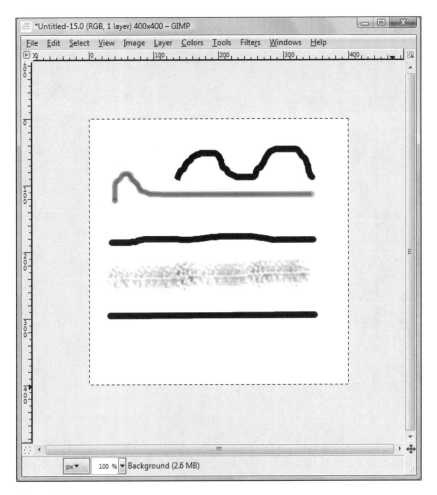

Figure 3.34
The Airbrush works similarly to the standard Paintbrush.

Selection Tools

Selection tools are designed to select regions from the active layer so that you can work on only the selected part of the image without affecting the unselected areas. There are several Selection tools, but for now it's important to understand their overall use as many of the features are all common.

Flood Fill Tool

The next tool we'll look at is the Flood Fill tool. It fills an area with a color, pattern, or gradient. You can use this to quickly fill the entire background of an image. You can also fill only a selection if you use the Selection tool.

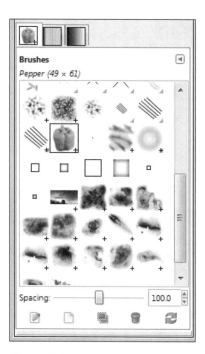

Figure 3.35
Brushes included with the GIMP.

Pencil Tool

The Pencil tool is used to draw lines with a hard edge and is very similar to the Paintbrush tool. However, there are differences between the tools; the Pencil tool is a hard-edged tool that does not perform anti-aliasing, whereas the Paintbrush tool is capable of it. That is, a Pencil tool will not produce fuzzy edges. There are times when you need hard edges, and others when the anti-aliasing is necessary. As an example, the Pencil tool works best if you are designing small graphics down to the pixel level. With the Paintbrush, pixel-level work is not consistent enough with the fuzzy edges it produces, and with the Pencil tool, you can be assured that it will do exactly as you instruct.

Additional Tools

There are many more tools available in GIMP and you are encouraged to spend time going through its help file. This chapter introduces you to some of the concepts of GIMP. When we later use it for creating graphics and textures, we'll do everything in a step-by-step system and cover the proper tools and their usage.

CHAPTER REVIEW

As you have seen throughout this chapter, GIMP offers a tremendous number of features and is easy for beginners to learn as the user interface can be mastered with relatively little effort. We have just touched on the absolute basics of this software and will later use it to create textures and 2D graphics for our game project. We also looked at the basic manipulation techniques for images, and now that you are familiar with graphics, you are ready to start the creation of content for a game. Before we move forward with graphics, we will create a proper game design in the next chapter, followed by our first look at the creation of music and sound effects. Once we are finished with those topics, we'll actually begin constructing the individual graphic components for the game.

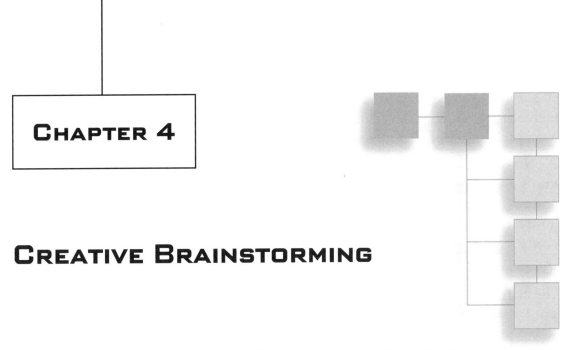

CHAPTER 4

CREATIVE BRAINSTORMING

Before we move on to building graphic components and music for our game, we have to decide what type of game to create, and how we are going to put it together. It's an important step that is often overlooked in the excitement of a game idea, especially when you are just starting out. Oftentimes, while creating a document, your game will take on a completely new direction because of things you discover while thinking through the game. Maybe you change the layout of the screen, or perhaps the game concept itself will actually change direction. Whatever it is you discover, saving yourself from starting and stopping projects will save you a great deal of time. While professional studios have huge design documents, for a one-man team it can be a much less intensive undertaking.

THE DESIGN DOCUMENT

As was already mentioned, a design document is often overlooked in the rush and excitement of a game idea. You might be thinking about skipping this step, but I would caution you about this. A poorly thought out game makes your life even more difficult when you try to build it. It's easier to change the concepts on paper than in coding and graphics, and the countless lost hours and frustration that will occur when doing so. The few hours you spend creating a thorough design document will actually save countless hours later down the development road. You might be lucky enough to create a very good quality game without a design document, but the key word in this is "luck." Most often, a game that begins without a properly developed design document will be delayed for months or may never be finished.

The creation of a design document is similar to the creation of a movie script. In it, you will write details of an exact story (if you have one—for example, a sports game would probably not have a story unless it was a sports game related to a particular player or set of circumstances such as a boxing career), an overview of the characters or opponents you intend to create, detailed descriptions of the levels, and so on.

It's worth noting that the design document is not something that needs to be chiseled into stone. That is, it can and should evolve as the game does, but it shouldn't be drastically altered. The design document will serve as a sort of road map to how the project will develop and should be as complete as possible. That being said, it can be changed when necessary to include a new character or a slight change in the plot.

Design Document Details

Now that you have a basic understanding of what a design document is, we need to look at the individual components or ideas that are included in it. Many larger game development teams will include information such as legalities, target audience, and market analysis for a game in their design document. While this works for larger teams, the lone-wolf developer doesn't really need to include all of the minor details and should instead focus on the main elements of the game.

Game Overview

This may be the most important piece of the entire document puzzle. Without a solid story or game overview, the later steps will be much more difficult to create. Be very thorough with the game overview. If you leave something out, go back and fix it immediately. Sometimes the smallest details can make a big difference in a large project.

Because you don't know exactly who will read this, make sure to use as many details as possible as you would if you were creating a good storybook. You would be surprised at the number of simple spelling errors that are present in most design documents. While everyone misses a word every now and then, you should try your best to keep grammar and spelling mistakes to a minimum. Some teams place background information in its own category, but because it relates to the story, it can be placed within the game overview category.

Levels

The next item you need to address is the levels that make up a game. If you do a thorough job in the preceding step, this one is very easy. You can create a list of levels, in the order in which they will be encountered in your game, adding any

Figure 4.1
A basic outline of a level for our space shooter game.

details you think are necessary. Some optional materials include ideas such as the layout of the level, a general description, or the placement of enemies to name a few. You can even attempt to create a mood or setting for your game.

The creation of a set of maps for the levels is helpful. They can be very detailed pictures, but more likely will be a set of simple lines, circles, and squares that form a rough layout of the levels. You can see an example of the space shooter that we are going to create in Figure 4.1. Don't worry about the actual graphics or the lack of quality in the graphics at this time; this information only serves as a basis for our game.

Game Characters

The next section of the design document deals with the characters that will be included in your game. Like the level area of the document, the character section should basically fall into place if the game overview is completed.

There are two basic types of characters in most games, a hero and enemies. You can include details of the hero such as any background information or some rough sketches. A list and description of animations should be included with every hero as well. Depending on their role in the story, you can also include descriptive ideas of their intelligence level and strength and basic information about how they react to the rest of the characters.

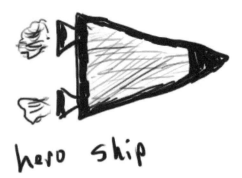

Figure 4.2
A rough sketch of a spaceship.

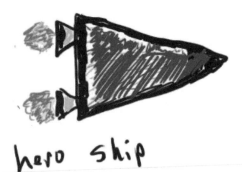

Figure 4.3
The spaceship with some color.

Once you finish with the heroes, you need to create a section for enemies you will encounter. This could include anything that will attack a player. For instance, in the space combat game we are creating, you could include an asteroid. You can follow the same basic procedures as the characters, making sure to include similar details and sketches where appropriate. For reference, Figures 4.2 through 4.4 contain sketches of the ship that we are using in our game project.

To finish the characters section of the design document, you need to include information about the types of weapons the characters will have access to. You should include detailed descriptions of every weapon that can be accessed by either type of character. You can also create a list that contains the damage that the weapon will create along with the type and amount of ammunition.

You'll notice the very simplistic sketches in this example. You can make them as detailed or as simple as you need. Often, it's more important to get them drawn than to worry about how great they look. You can always go back to them and clean them up later.

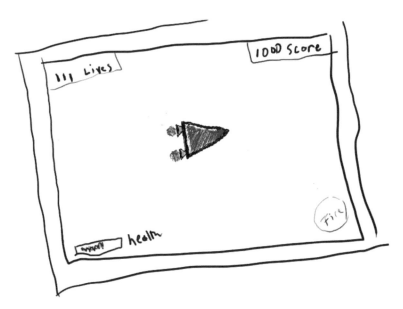

Figure 4.4
The ship placed on our level.

Menus and Navigation

The creation of a list that details menu navigation is very important. It helps you keep track of how the game is linked, something that is obviously emphasized when you are dealing with smaller screens. You don't have much room from error when you are limited to the real estate available on the iPhone so you need to pay particular attention to this step. You should create the main menu and a simple illustration of how the screens will be linked together. Nothing fancy is necessary, but all of the menus should be included. For example, you could use something like Figure 4.6 to display information about the opening screen of our space shooter game.

User Interface

The user interface goes hand in hand with the menu navigation system. For convenience, you could place them under the same category; they deal with many of the same ideas. The description for this category can be text-based information about what you are planning to do, but ideally, sketches work the best. Like most of the design document, they don't have to be fancy, but details are important.

Music and Sound Effects

This section is key. You can discuss the possibilities of tools that you plan to employ, the types of sound effects that you have in mind for some of the game, and possibly detail the music you might have in the levels that you listed earlier in the process. For instance, you should decide if you are going to use MIDI (Musical Instrument Digital

Weapons	Info/Damage
Basic Laser	Beginning Weapon Light Damage
Upgraded Laser	Medium Damage Picked up when reached level 3.
Guided Missle	High Damage Available Randomly when score reaches 5000.

Figure 4.5
List of weapons and damages.

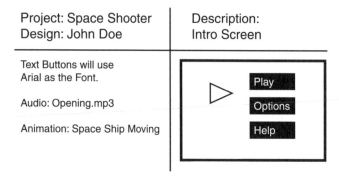

Figure 4.6
The screen layout from the space shooter game.

Interface), WAV (Waveform Audio File Format), or MP3 files for the music, and if you'll need things like explosions or footsteps for sound effects. You've probably heard about MP3s already. MIDI is a protocol for recording and playing back music using digital synthesizers, and WAV is a specific audio format created by Microsoft and IBM. You should also list the genres of music you'll be planning such as rock, pop, and country to name a few.

Single or Multi-Player

The next step focuses on the game play itself, and specifically, if it's a single or multi-player game. For example, if you are planning a First-Person Shooter (FPS), you might decide that it will be both a multi-player and single-player game. If you are

Figure 4.7
A user interface example.

doing a puzzle game, you may only need to have single-player support. Sometimes the information in this area of the document is discussed in other areas, but you shouldn't worry about duplication of ideas. This is especially true on a first draft as you can always change the document after a later inspection.

If it's a single-player game, you can describe the game experience in a few sentences and perhaps break down some of the key elements of the single-player game. For example, you could begin by setting up the location of the game. Next, you could detail the types of enemies you'll be facing and the route to complete the game (for example, you need to finish 10 levels before the game is over). You could also list how the game ends for common situations like not completing a level on time or being struck by an enemy's bullet. Another idea that you can include is a projection on the number of hours the game is going to take before a player finishes and how the player ultimately win the game. A single-player game is usually easier to not only design, but also to discuss in the design document.

A multi-player game description begins the same way as a single player. You can take a few sentences to describe the basics of the game play. For example, if you were creating a basketball game, it could be a street ball, college, professional, or international rules game. You can also decide what types of options you'll have, such as franchise mode for a professional game or what types of parks you'll include for a street ball game. Now is a good time to decide how many players will be allowed to play simultaneously and how you plan to implement the client-server or peer-to-peer system. In this basketball example, you need to decide how many people you'll allow to play on the same team. It's best if you have the exact technical ideas listed, but it isn't always necessary, especially when you are doing a first draft.

Miscellaneous

The final area of the document is for miscellaneous information that may be specific to a certain type of genre or doesn't fit neatly into another category. You can name this category anything that works well for you. For example, suppose you decided to create a basketball street game and you wanted to include information about the way the basketball players will dress so that you can keep track of players from both teams. You could have one team play in white shirts and another in red shirts. If you have multiple additions, you should split them up into multiple categories to keep everything easy to read and follow. The miscellaneous section is a good place to include items such as sketches or concept drawings. This way, you can refer to the miscellaneous section instead of cluttering up your text.

Required Resources and Scheduling

The final area that you should be sure to include is the required resources and scheduling information. The schedule should include an estimate for the completion of a final project along with specific steps that should be reached along the way, such as an alpha or beta product.

CHAPTER REVIEW

Although we have gone over this process in some detail, we are only really scratching the surface. There are entire volumes of books written on much of the information we have briefly covered. That being said, with the material from this chapter, you shouldn't have a problem creating a functional design document for your game. Don't get offended if someone suggests that you change or alter something in the document. The input from others is important to the process and the information you receive is usually invaluable. It's important to look at the creation of this document as an inexact science.

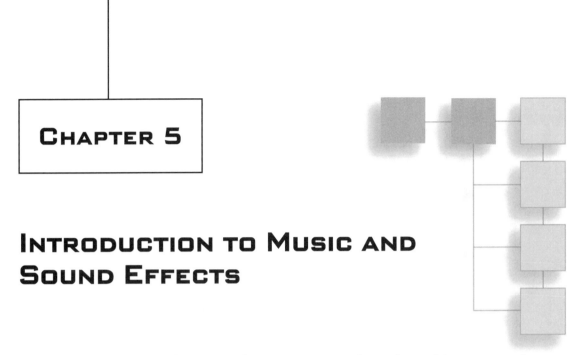

CHAPTER 5

INTRODUCTION TO MUSIC AND SOUND EFFECTS

Although having a good concept for your game and good graphics are very important components in the game development process, it's not enough in a competitive marketplace. To have a completely successful game, music and sound effects should convey information that helps set up a level without being overwhelming to a player.

In this chapter, we'll be introduced to Sony's ACID Xpress, which we'll use to create music. We will refer to the software as ACID throughout the remaining chapters of the book. In the next chapter, we'll look at Audacity software for the creation of sound effects.

GETTING TO KNOW ACID

ACID is undoubtedly the easiest to use loop-based music creation tool ever created, and it can be utilized in many game development projects. It is called loop-based software because it uses small loops of various sounds that can be combined to create some amazing music productions. As far as software goes, it is undoubtedly one of the easiest tools to use.

INSTALLATION

Before we begin discussing the specifics of ACID, we need to install it. It's located at http://www.acidplanet.com/downloads/xpress/. At the time of this writing, it was at version 7, but you can visit the site to download the most up-to-date version

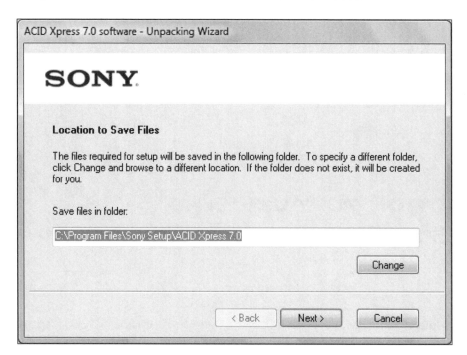

Figure 5.1
The installation program begins with this screen.

currently available. You must register for an account on the site to access the free version or trial of the full version of ACID.

After downloading, the first step in the installation process is to run the executable file. It will begin the installation process; you will be presented with a screen that looks similar to Figure 5.1. To continue the installation, click Next. You don't need to change the default folder locations.

When you click the Next button, the files begin extracting, as you can see in Figure 5.2.

Depending on your PC, you might need to install additional components; an example is shown in Figure 5.3.

Once finished, a dialog similar to the one shown in Figure 5.4 will appear; you can click the OK button to continue.

From the next screen, which can be seen in Figure 5.5, click the Next button, which will then display the ACID license agreement (see Figure 5.6). Read through the agreement and then click the Next button. You will be given a choice to change the path of the install. Unless you have a particular reason for doing so, leave the settings as is.

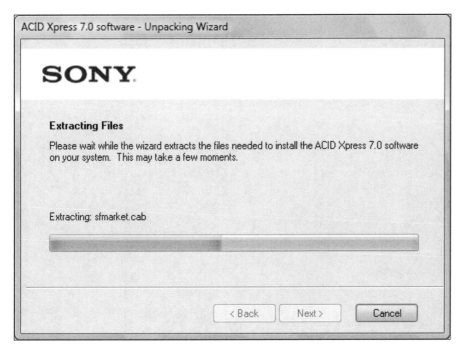

Figure 5.2
Files are extracting to the folder location.

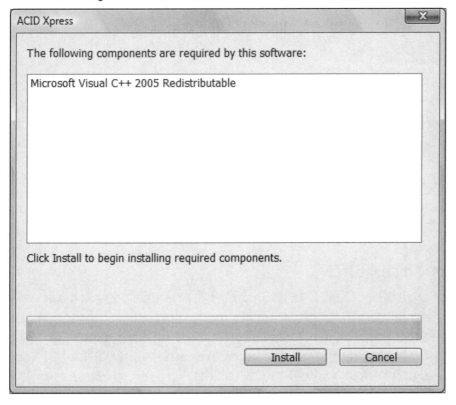

Figure 5.3
To finish the install, additional components may need to be installed.

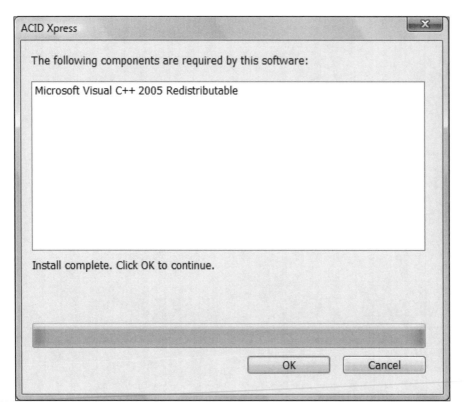

Figure 5.4
The components are finished installing.

If you click the Next button, the installation program will continue with your final prompt, from which you can click the Install button. It may take some time to finish the installation, and once complete, select the Finish button. At this time, you can open ACID by choosing it from the Start button.

Click on the Finish button to run ACID for the first time. You should see a window similar to Figure 5.7.

INTRODUCTION TO ACID

One of the greatest attributes of ACID is an interface that is quick to learn and very easy to master. It's a great choice for game development, especially for those who are in charge of creating the graphics, development, and music for your game. For those with a music background, ACID becomes another extremely powerful tool in your arsenal of choices, and for those without any music background, there are royalty-free loops that you can use to create music.

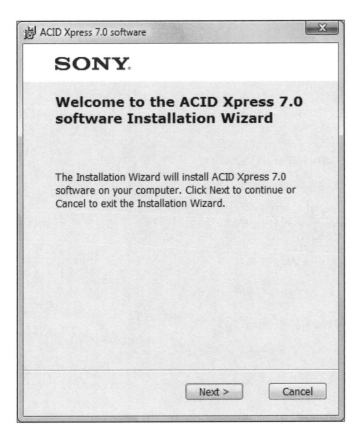

Figure 5.5
Your installation screen should look similar to this.

The Interface

To begin, let's look at the screen and identify the various elements that make up the ACID window. At the top of the window, which you can see in Figure 5.8, you will see a familiar Windows title and menu bars. Below that is a toolbar that gives you quick access to the most commonly used commands. These tools can be used to edit, play back, and save your composition. We'll look at these tools in more depth later in this chapter.

In Figure 5.9, you can see four main areas labeled. First, in the upper-left portion of the screen, you can see the ACID Track List. To its right, you will find the Track View, and at the bottom, you will see the Multi-Function area. The Multi-Function area contains the Media Explorer and Properties window. (ACID Pro contains additional windows but we won't cover them here.) Finally, along the bottom of the window you will see the Status bar, which displays useful information like available system memory.

Figure 5.6
The license agreement for ACID.

Changing or Adjusting the Interface

You can resize the main windows that make up the interface. For instance, you could lengthen the Track List, Track View, or Multi-Function section. To try this, place your mouse over a border between the Track List and Multi-Function sections and then click and drag to the top. You will see the windows change. When you want to stop, simply release the mouse button. Once you have the windows how you like them, ACID will automatically remember the settings every time you open it.

The Media Explorer

The Media Explorer is very much like the standard Windows Explorer. On the left is a directory view of the drives on your computer and drives on the network if you are connected to a network. When you click on a drive or a folder in a drive, you will see the contents displayed on the right. Click on the plus (+) to the right of the C: drive

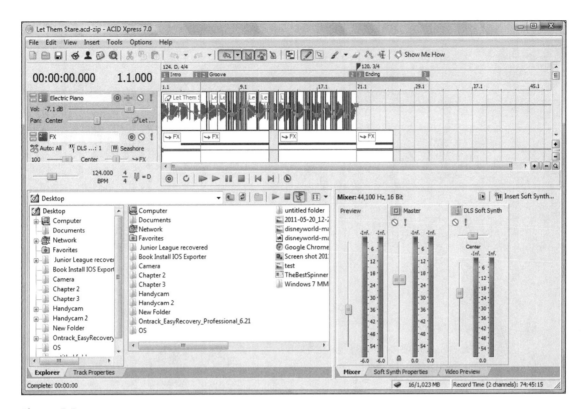

Figure 5.7
The ACID interface is displayed.

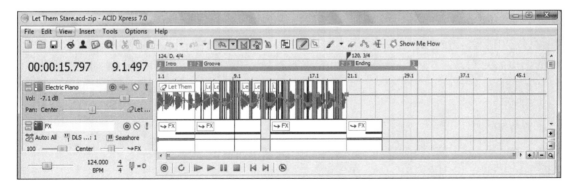

Figure 5.8
The ACID interface has standard elements.

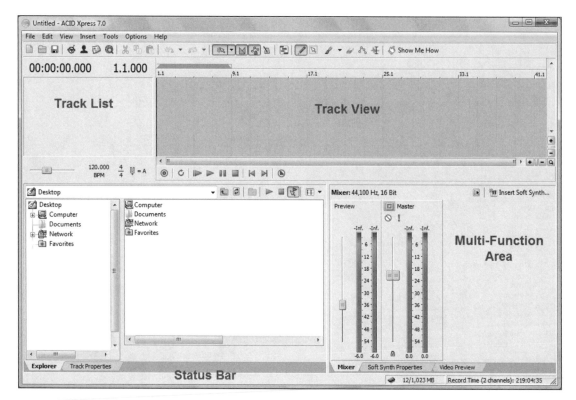

Figure 5.9
The ACID interface with labels.

icon to display the contents of your computer hard drive. You can see an example of this in Figure 5.10.

You use the Media Explorer to locate and find tracks that you would like to add to your project. Once they are located, you can simply double-click them or drag them to the Track View or Track List.

The Timeline

The Timeline is part of the Track View and is used to create the project. By "drawing" the tracks in the timeline, you are able to compose a track. Figure 5.11 contains a labeled drawing for the Track View window.

Beat Ruler   The Beat Ruler is displayed along the top of the Track View and allows you to place events in reference to the musical time of bars and beats. The timeline is fixed length and will not change when you alter the tempo. In Figure 5.12, the 1.1 represents beat 1 of measure 1, and each ruler mark represents one beat.

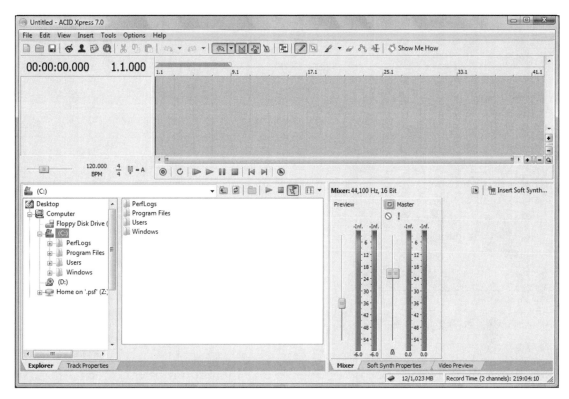

Figure 5.10
The Media Explorer works similarly to Windows Explorer.

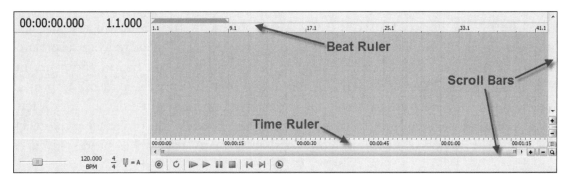

Figure 5.11
The Track View is made up of the space where you will draw events on each track.

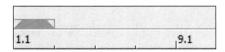

Figure 5.12
Close-up of the Beat Ruler.

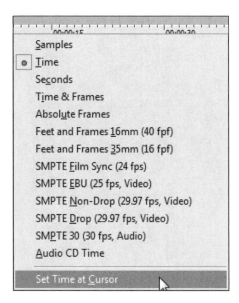

Figure 5.13
Right-clicking the Time Ruler changes the format.

Time Ruler The Time Ruler is displayed along the bottom of the Track View. To change the format of the display, right-click on the timeline (see Figure 5.13) and choose an option from the shortcut menu. The tempo changes the number of bars and beats per second, which will change your timeline.

Scroll Bars The horizontal scroll bar is displayed below the Time Ruler. Click and drag the scroll bar to pan left or right through the project. The scroll bar also functions as a zoom control. Click and drag the edges of the scroll bar to zoom in and out, or double-click the scroll bar to zoom out so that the entire length of the project will be displayed, The vertical scroll bar is displayed on the right side of Track View. Click and drag the scroll bar to pan up and down through the project. Double-click the scroll bar to zoom the project out so that as many tracks will be displayed as possible.

Zoom Control The magnifying glass icon displayed at the ends of the scroll bars allow you to change the magnification level of your ACID project and can be seen in Figure 5.14.

Track List The Track List contains the master controls for each track. From here you can adjust the volume, mute the track, and reorder tracks. You can see a sample of the Track List in Figure 5.15.

Figure 5.14
The zoom control.

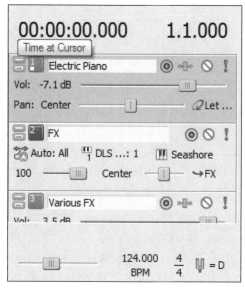

Figure 5.15
The Track List gives you control over each of the tracks.

There are a few areas within the Track List that we should look at further. The volume and pan drop-down control, which can be seen in Figure 5.16, is very useful. It allows you to alter the volume and/or the pan of a track. By selecting volume from the list, you can determine how loud a track is in the mix. A value of 0 dB means that the track is played with no boost or cut from ACID. Clicking and dragging the fader (which is directly to the right of the drop-down) to the left decreases the volume while clicking and dragging to the right boosts the volume.

Figure 5.16
The volume controls how loud a track is in a mix.

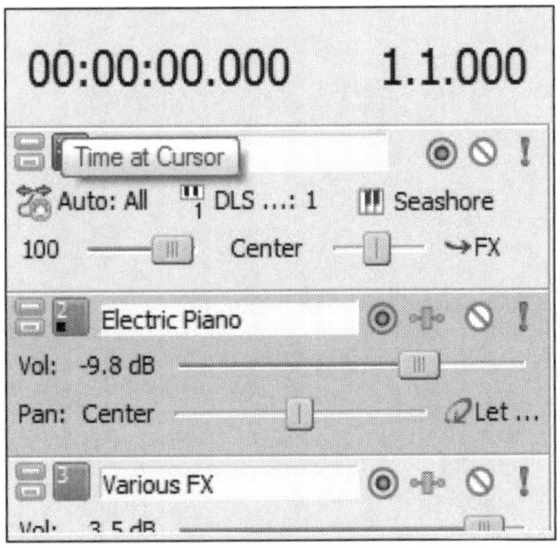

Figure 5.17
Moving the top track.

Pan controls the position of a track in a stereo field. Clicking and dragging the fader to the left will place the track in the left speaker more than the right, while moving the fader to the right will place the track in the right speaker.

Another thing that the Track List is used for is the placement of tracks. They can be moved around to create logical groupings at any time during a project's creation. To do so, click on its icon in the Track List and drag it to a new location. While dragging it, a new location is indicated by a highlighted line separating the tracks, a sample of which can be seen in Figure 5.17, after we have moved the top track. You can move multiple tracks by using Shift or Control to highlight them before dragging.

Lastly, you can rename a track using the Track List by clicking inside the track label. Renaming a track applies to the project only, and does not change the file associated with a track. Figure 5.18 displays a track being renamed.

Figure 5.18
The track is being renamed within the project.

CHAPTER REVIEW

As you have seen, there are a tremendous number of features in ACID that make it an extremely useful program for game developers. It's one of the easiest programs that you'll ever use and one that you will undoubtedly make a spot for in your tool-box. In the next chapter, we'll look at the open-source program called Audacity, the software that we'll use to create sound effects and edit individual tracks for use in ACID. Later, we'll use ACID to create the music for a game.

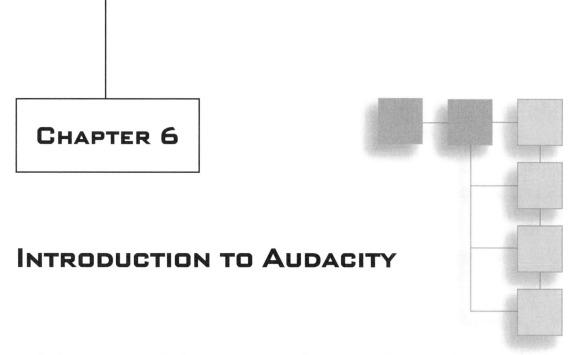

CHAPTER 6

INTRODUCTION TO AUDACITY

In the last chapter, we looked at ACID, which is going to be our application of choice for the creation of music for our game. In this chapter, we are going to look at Audacity, a program that we'll use for recording and editing sound effects for our game.

INSTALLING AUDACITY

Before we begin discussing the specifics of Audacity, we need to install it. You can download the most up-to-date version of Audacity from http://audacity.sourceforge. com. Once you download the file, you can begin the first step of the installation process by running the executable file. You will be presented with a screen that looks similar to Figure 6.1. To continue the installation, click the OK button.

The welcome screen shown in Figure 6.2 will appear. From this screen, click Next.

The next screen, which appears in Figure 6.3, is the license agreement for the software. The software is released as open source, but it's a good idea to review the terms. Then click the Next button.

From the screen that is shown in Figure 6.4, choose the default installation location. Leave as is unless you have a particular need to change it and then click the Next button to continue.

Your installation window should look similar to Figure 6.5. Click the Install button to continue. Audacity will now be installed.

Figure 6.1
The installation program begins with this screen.

Figure 6.2
Click Next from the welcome screen.

Figure 6.6 displays the final license agreement. You should read the document and then click the OK button to continue.

The final step of the installation of Audacity is shown in Figure 6.7. Click Finish to end the setup and launch Audacity, which is shown in Figure 6.8.

AUDACITY'S INTERFACE

Like ACID in the previous chapter, we'll now look at the user interface and some basic operations of Audacity. In the next chapter, we'll use it to edit sound effects for our game.

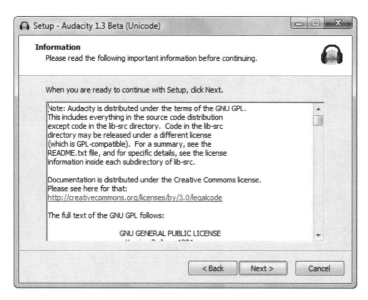

Figure 6.3
The license agreement.

Figure 6.4
You can change the installation location.

To begin, let's look at the screen and identify the various elements that make up the Audacity interface, which can be seen in Figure 6.8. At the top of the window, you will see a familiar Windows title and menu bars. Below that is a toolbar that gives you quick access to the most commonly used commands. These tools can be used to edit, play back, and save your composition.

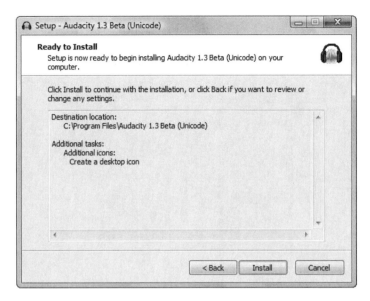

Figure 6.5
You are now ready to install.

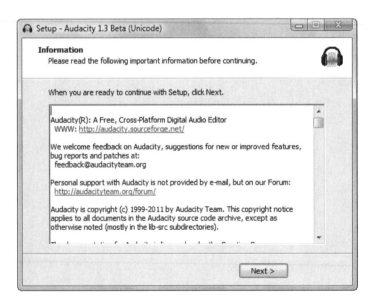

Figure 6.6
The Audacity license agreement is next.

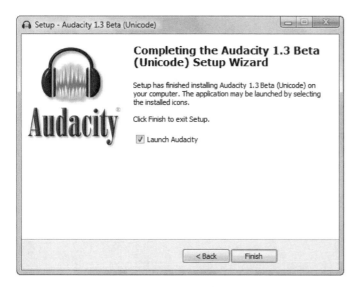

Figure 6.7
The final step of the installation.

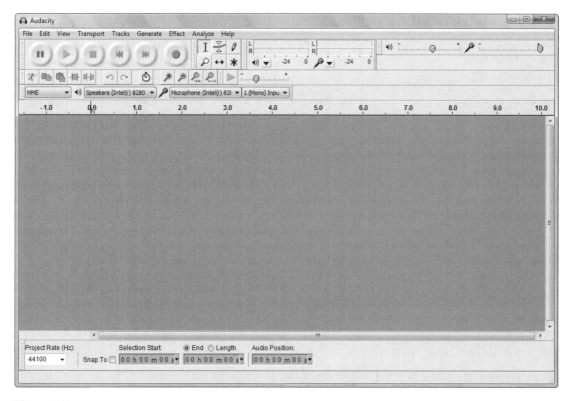

Figure 6.8
The Audacity interface.

Figure 6.9
The toolbars contain shortcuts to common functions.

Figure 6.10
The Transport Toolbar comprises a number of buttons for playback.

Menu and Toolbars

The Audacity menu, seen in Figure 6.9, contains shortcuts to common functions like file opening and saving.

Transport Toolbar

The Transport Toolbar can be seen in Figure 6.10. It includes playback, stop, and record controls as well as buttons to skip to the front or end of a file.

Tools Toolbar

The Tools Toolbar, seen in Figure 6.11, contains several editing-related tools including the Selection tool, which allows you to click to select a start point for audio playback, or click and drag to select a range of audio to play or edit. The Envelope tool allows smooth volume changes over the length of a track. The Draw tool allows you to adjust the volume level of individual audio samples. The Zoom tool does just what its name suggests: allows you to zoom in and out. Time Shift lets you synchronize audio in a project by dragging individual or multiple tracks or clips left or right along the timeline.

Meter Toolbar

The Meter Toolbar can be seen in Figure 6.12, and displays the amplitude of audio that is being played, or recorded, in the current project. It is an easy way to see if the

Figure 6.11
Audacity's Tools Toolbar contains editing tools.

Figure 6.12
The Meter Toolbar is useful for controlling clipping.

Figure 6.13
The Mixer Toolbar controls playback and recording volume.

audio is clipped, which means that it is too loud and will be displayed as a flat top rather than a peak. Clipping is important to control as it results in distortion.

Mixer Toolbar

The Mixer Toolbar is used in conjunction with the Meter Toolbar and is used to control the playback and recording volume. As you can see in Figure 6.13, you can also select the input source here.

Edit Toolbar

The Edit Toolbar, shown in Figure 6.14, is more for convenience than anything else. You can find all of the same tools in the Edit Toolbar that you can in the menus such as Copy, Cut, and Paste to name a few.

Transcription Toolbar

The Transcription Toolbar, shown in Figure 6.15, has a Play-at-Speed button that plays audio at the speed set by the Play-at-Speed slider that is located to its right. Playback can be paused and resumed at the adjusted speed.

Figure 6.14
Like its name suggests, the Edit Toolbar contains editing tools.

Figure 6.15
You can change playback speed with the Transcription Toolbar.

Figure 6.16
The Device Toolbar preferences.

Figure 6.17
Timeline can have different values depending on the zoom level.

Device Toolbar

The Device Toolbar provides an easy way to select the combination of interface host and sound device that Audacity will use for both playback and recording. You can do this without having to open the Device Preferences. The Device Toolbar can be seen in Figure 6.16.

Timeline

In Audacity, the Timeline (see Figure 6.17) is a horizontal ruler above the tracks that measures time in the track. Depending on your level of zoom, the ruler may span several minutes of audio or only a few seconds.

Tracks Display

The Tracks area of the interface in Audacity is the area in which you view your audio material in the form of a waveform. You can use your mouse in the Waveform Display to select data and manipulate it using the various tools we have discussed. You can see the Tracks display in Figure 6.18.

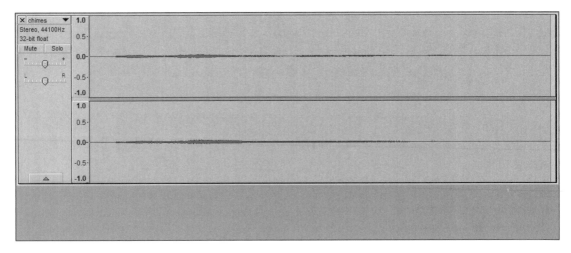

Figure 6.18
Tracks are seen as waveforms.

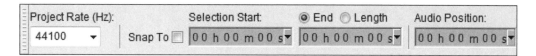

Figure 6.19
The Selection Toolbar at the bottom of the window.

Selection Toolbar

By default, the Selection Toolbar is displayed at the very bottom of the Audacity interface (see Figure 6.19). The Selection Toolbar includes the Project Rate and Snap To controls. It also lets you precisely place the cursor point or selection region without having to click or drag in the waveform using a mouse, and without having to zoom in first to find the exact spot.

CHAPTER REVIEW

In this chapter we looked at many of the basics of Audacity, an open-source audio editor that we'll use for creating and editing sound effects. In addition to learning the basic features of the software, we also learned about many of the features and tools that make Audacity so popular. In the next chapter, we'll begin constructing the graphics that we'll use in our game.

CHAPTER 7

CREATING GRAPHICS FOR OUR GAME

Up to this point, we've covered theories and tools, but not much in the way of practical hands-on creation. That's about to change. In this chapter, you'll learn how to create a spaceship for your game, a very cool-looking space background, and a few other miscellaneous items like exhaust and lasers.

SPACE BACKGROUND

If you can think back to the very basic drawings from our design document in Chapter 4, you will remember that our game has a backdrop that looks like space. The environment wasn't really covered in great detail, but it will be a complete backdrop with stars and a planet. We will begin by opening GIMP and changing the Foreground Color to Black, as shown in Figure 7.1.

Next, create a new image by choosing the File > New menu. Click the Advanced Options button, set the image to 480 × 320 pixels, and choose Fill With: Foreground Color. You can see these settings in Figure 7.2.

You should now have an image that looks like Figure 7.3—just a simple black rectangle. Let's add some stars to liven it up. Select Filters > Noise > Hurl, and from the resulting dialog box select Randomize and then click the OK button. The filter should look like Figure 7.4.

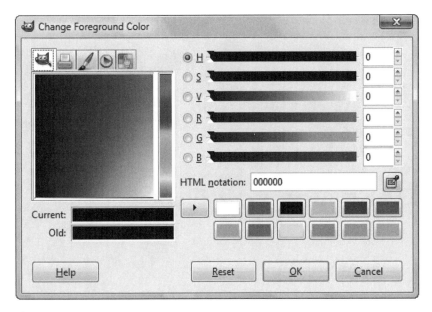

Figure 7.1
The color needs to be set as follows.

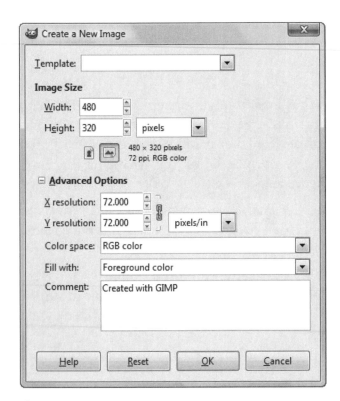

Figure 7.2
Basic settings for our backdrop.

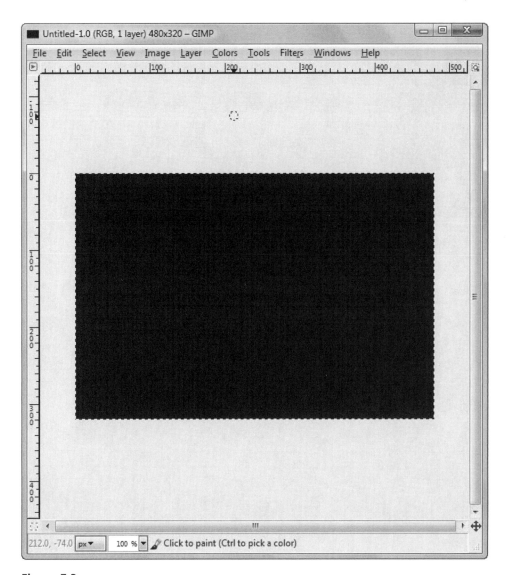

Figure 7.3
The image should look like a simple black rectangle.

The image looks like a mess right now (see Figure 7.5), but don't worry, as it won't be like this for too long. To remove any colors from the filtered stars, simply click Colors > Desaturate and then click the OK button (Figure 7.6). We could always add in color later if desired, but I don't think we'll need to for this project. Next, to

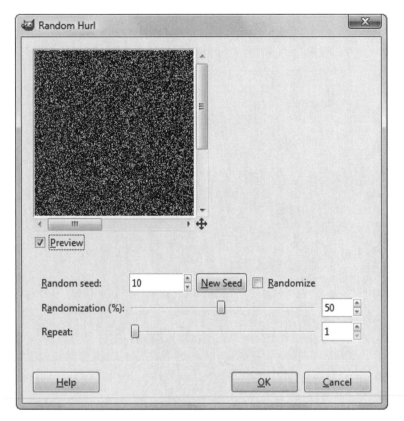

Figure 7.4
The filter settings to create some stars.

thin out the dots and create an environment that looks more like "stars," choose Colors > Levels. In the first text box, enter a number close to 230 (Figure 7.7), which will get us a medium-density star field. Refer to Figure 7.8 for a representation of the space scene at this time.

The stars look pretty good now, but we can improve them by choosing Filters > Light and Shadow > Sparkle (Figure 7.9). From the Filter window, you can set Flare Intensity to about .15 for a fairly subtle sparkle effect and then click OK (Figure 7.10). The stars are now finished and you can save the image by choosing File > Save and naming it Background.xcf.

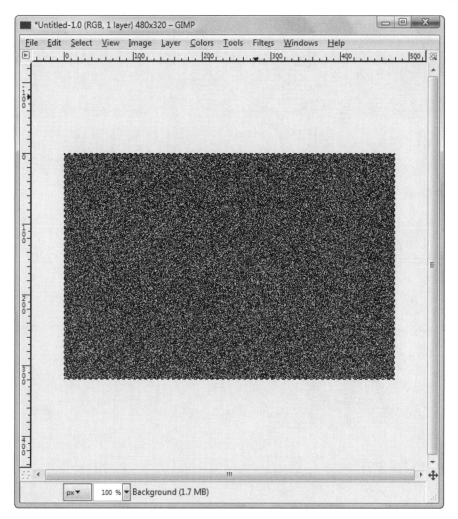

Figure 7.5
The image doesn't look too great so far.

Figure 7.6
We just need a black-and-white image right now.

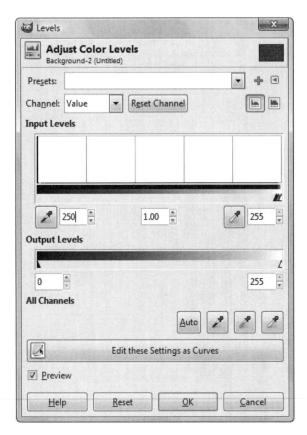

Figure 7.7
Thinning out the stars so they look realistic.

Creating a Planet

We've gotten our stars finished, and they look okay, but it would be nice to put some additional features into the background. Select File > New Image and create a file that is 240 × 240, as seen in Figure 7.11.

Open the Channels tab dialog box on the right side of the GIMP in the Layers, Channels, Paths dialog box, right-click and select New Channel. Name it "alpha1." You can see an example of this dialog box in Figure 7.12.

Next, choose Filter > Render > Clouds > Plasma (Figure 7.13) and then click OK.

We need to add some "texture" to the object, so select Filters > Map > Bump Map, like you can see in Figure 7.14. In the dialog box, select the item that has "alpha 1" in

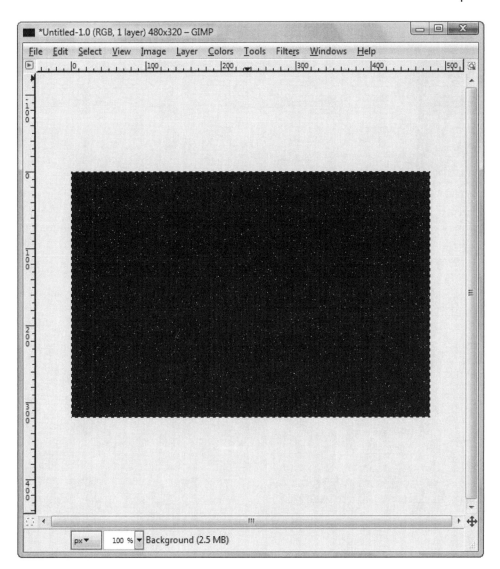

Figure 7.8
Our stars are nearly complete.

the drop-down list and also make sure to set all options as seen in Figure 7.14, such as "sinear" in the drop-down list, and then click OK.

You can be creative at this stage and pick whatever color of planet you would like to create by choosing Colors > Color Balance and setting colors like those shown in Figure 7.15. When you click OK, your image will look like a color version of Figure 7.16.

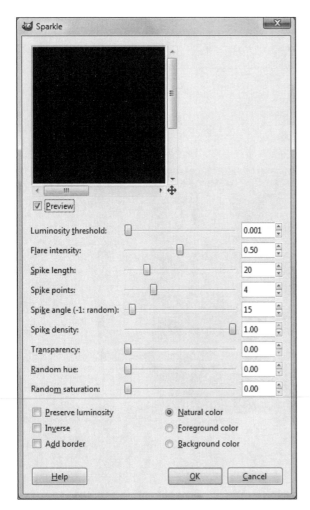

Figure 7.9
The sparkle filter options.

We can't really have a square planet floating around, so to make it look spherical, you can click Filters > Light And Shadow >Apply Lens. Choose Set Surroundings to Background Color (you can see this in Figure 7.17) and click OK. The planet is rather odd looking in Figure 7.18.

We need to remove the outer areas, as the planet doesn't look right at this time. Begin by choosing Layer > Transparency > Add New Alpha Channel as can be seen in Figure 7.19.

With the Fuzzy Select tool, hold down your Shift key and click in the four outer areas that will be in the four corners of the planet, as shown in Figure 7.20. With

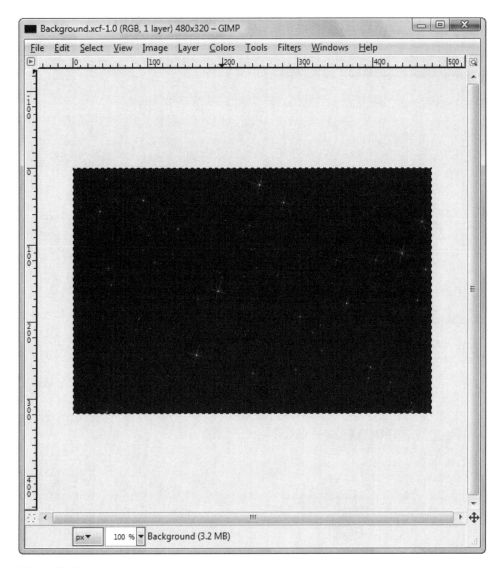

Figure 7.10
Your image should look something like this after adding sparkle.

the selections made, choose Clear from the Edit menu and you will be left with Figure 7.21.

Next, we need to create a shadow to make the planet look a little more interesting. We can begin by creating a new layer above the planet (Figure 7.22), and then choosing the Ellipse tool. Drag a box from one corner of your image to the other, creating a circle roughly the same size as the planet. Use the Bucket Fill tool to fill in this selection with solid black (Figure 7.23).

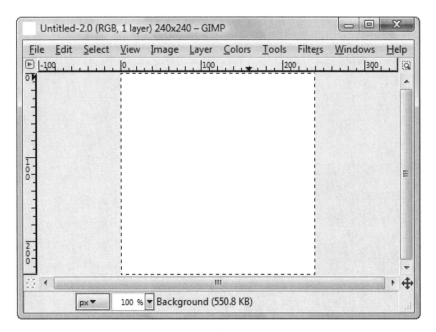

Figure 7.11
A new image for our planet.

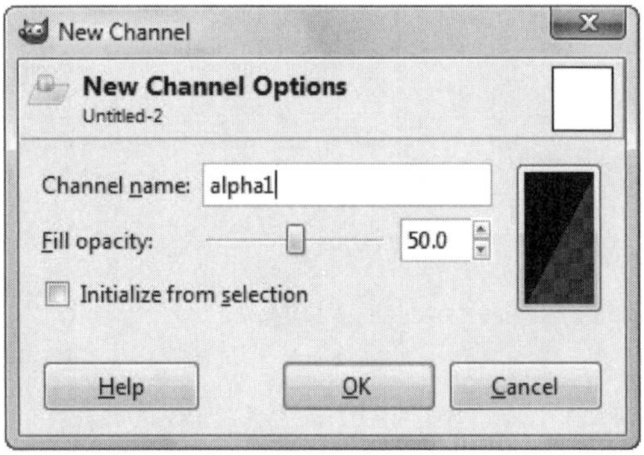

Figure 7.12
Creating a new alpha channel.

Next, click Layer and choose Scale Layer to increase the shadow layer to about 125%–150% of its current size. The entire image will appear black but it's temporary. Use the Move tool to position it similarly to Figure 7.24. As this is about art, and not an exact science, play around with the locations to get the look that you like.

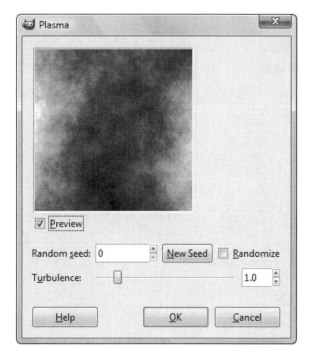

Figure 7.13
Another filter makes our job easier.

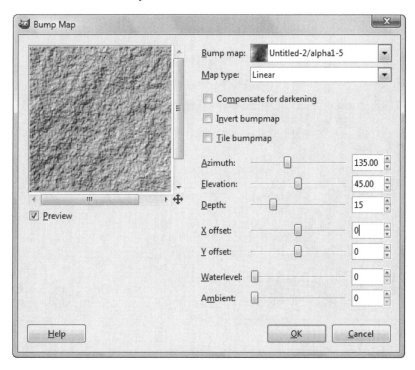

Figure 7.14
Make sure your settings look like this.

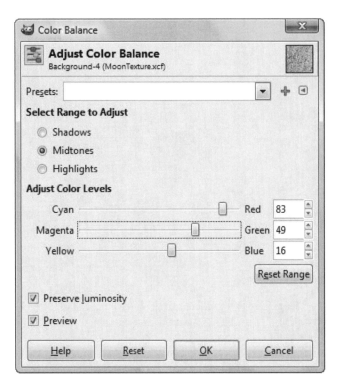

Figure 7.15
Adding color to the image.

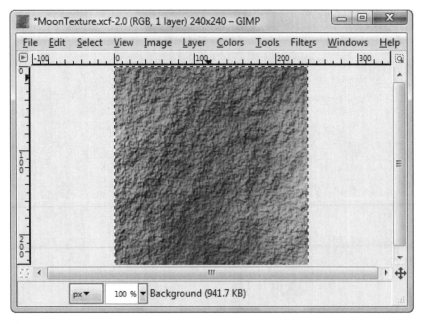

Figure 7.16
Our planet is just at the beginning of its creation.

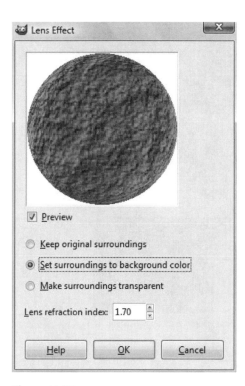

Figure 7.17
Settings for the filter.

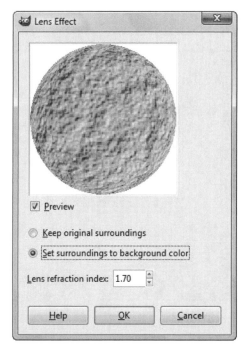

Figure 7.18
The planet needs some more work.

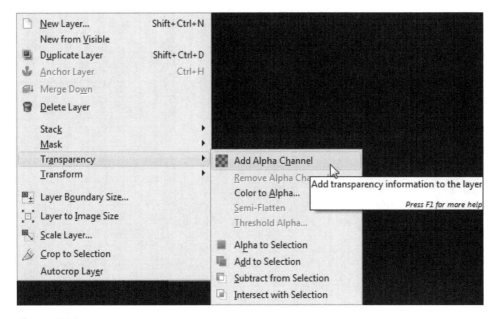

Figure 7.19
A new alpha channel being added to the project.

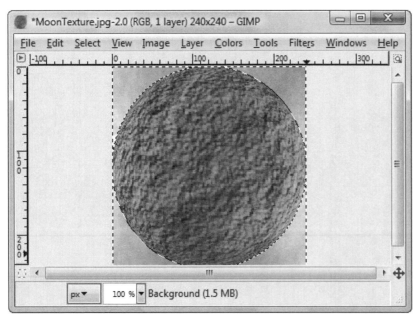

Figure 7.20
Using the Fuzzy Select tool to get the areas outside of the sphere.

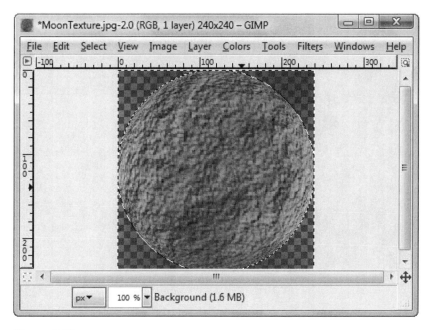

Figure 7.21
The areas removed.

Figure 7.22
A new layer added to the project.

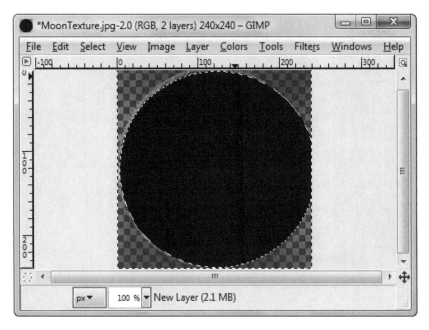

Figure 7.23
Filling the circle with the color black.

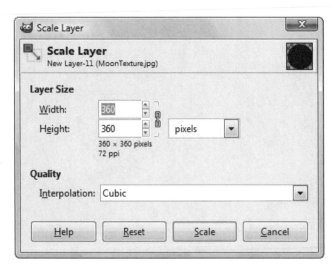

Figure 7.24
Positioning the selection that will become a shadow.

Once you have a position you are happy with, click Filters > Blur > Gaussian Blur. Set the value to about 250, as seen in Figure 7.25. You can now save this image as Moon.png. Be sure to use a PNG file; we need that because of the alpha channel.

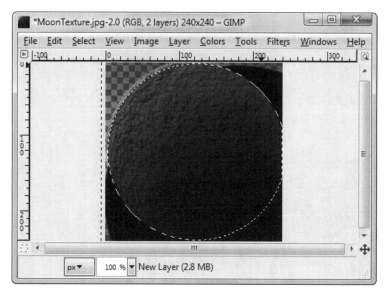

Figure 7.25
Our planet is finished.

Adding Planet to Background

Now that our planet is finished, let's add it back to the original work. Open the original background and choose File > Open As Layer, as shown in Figure 7.26.

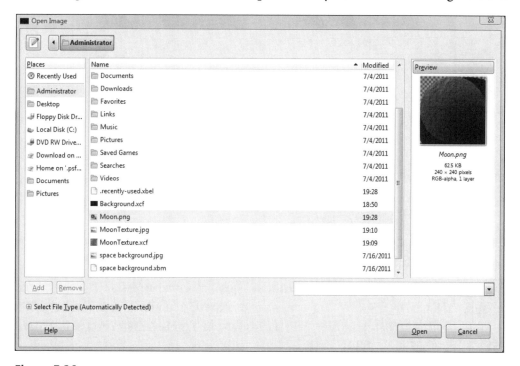

Figure 7.26
Open the file as a layer.

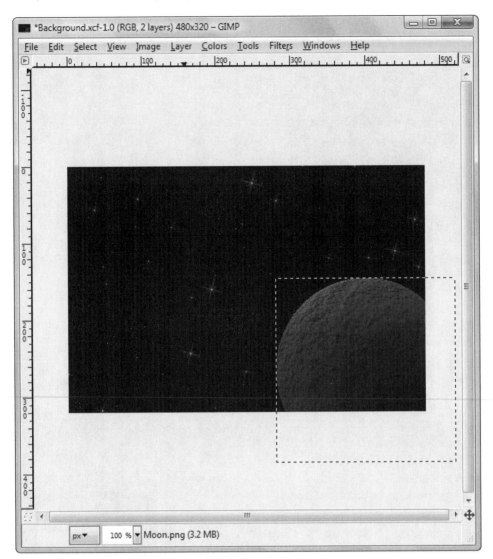

Figure 7.27
You can position the planet using this as a rough guide for placement.

Using the Move tool, position the planet at lower left of the background, and again, you can place it where you feel comfortable with something similar to Figure 7.27.

It looks pretty good, but it would be nice to add a "nebula" effect to make it even better. For this nebula effect, start by creating a new transparent Nebula layer (Figure 7.28). Next, pick Filters > Render > Clouds > Plasma, shown in Figure 7.29. Then select Randomize and click OK (Figure 7.30).

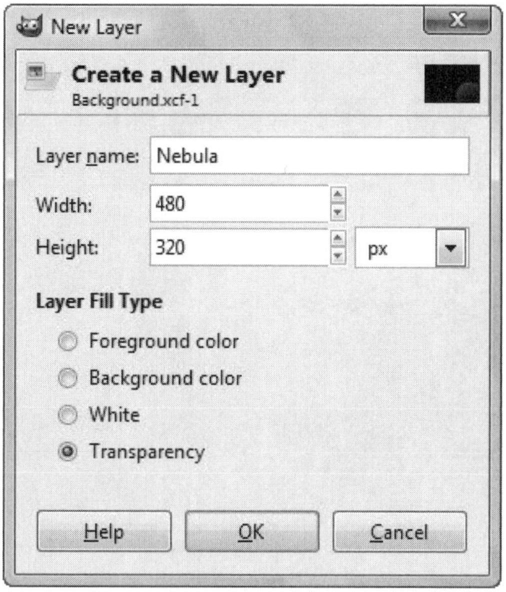

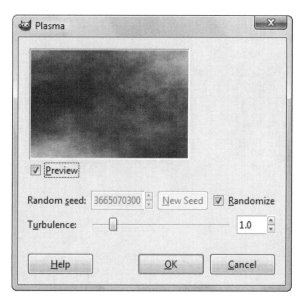

Figure 7.28
A nebula layer.

Figure 7.29
Using the Plasma filter.

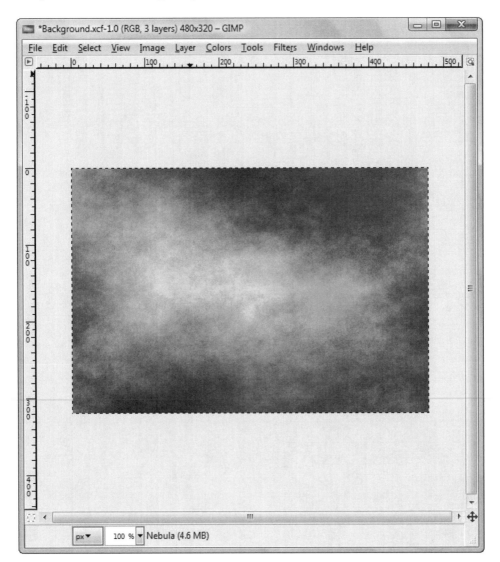

Figure 7.30
Colors are all over the place right now.

Let's alter these colors slightly by using Filters > Blur > Motion Blur. You can see the values and settings in Figure 7.31.

We are left with only a few minor details to finish this. First, adjust the transparency of the Layer to a value that you like. For starters, you can refer to Figure 7.32.

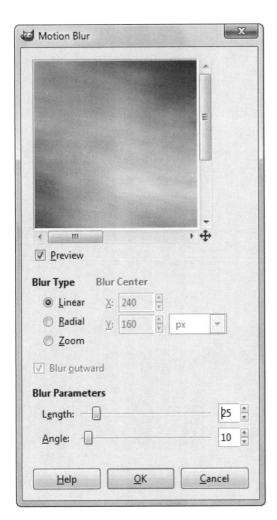

Figure 7.31
Motion Blur will take away some blockiness.

For one final added touch, add a new Layer to the project called Nova. Next, choose Filter > Light and Shadow > Supernova. Adjust the position, using Figure 7.33 as a rough guide, to the position that you would like, choose a radius around 5 and spokes around 40, and then click OK. Your final scene will look something like Figure 7.34. Congratulations, you have finished the first background and can now save the image. You can see how easy it would be to create hundreds of variations of this background by moving the Supernova and changing the colors and transparency of

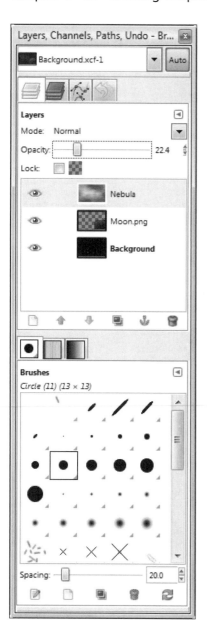

Figure 7.32
Changing the transparency of the layer.

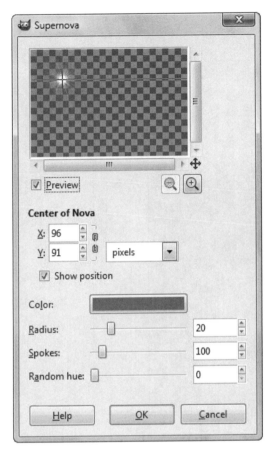

Figure 7.33
Use this as a guide for placement.

some of the layers. This is an easy technique to create different-looking levels for a game.

DRAWING A SPACESHIP

Now that we have a background for our game, we need to focus on creating a spaceship that will be used as the "hero" in our game. To begin, open the GIMP if it is not already open and create a new 32 × 32 image like the one shown in Figure 7.35.

When you create such a small image, chances are it will look very small on your screen. In order to make our drawing easier, we need to resize the window and zoom in until you are able to clearly see the area, as in Figure 7.36.

Figure 7.34
Your final scene.

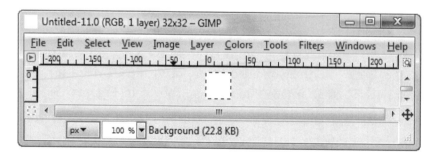

Figure 7.35
A new image is necessary for our ship.

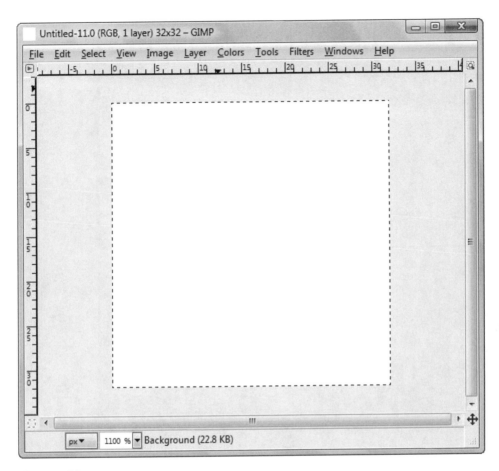

Figure 7.36
The area is zoomed in.

We want the spaceship to be symmetrical, and to help us accomplish this, we will drag guides to the center of the image by clicking on the ruler that is positioned to the left of the image and dragging it to the right. You can position it at 16, which is exactly half of the 32-pixel image we created. Do the same for top to bottom, and again position it at 16 so that you can create your spaceship in the center of the canvas. Figure 7.37 shows the guides as drawn.

Use the Ellipse Select tool and draw an ellipse that stretches nearly across the entire image like Figure 7.38. This will be the main body of the image.

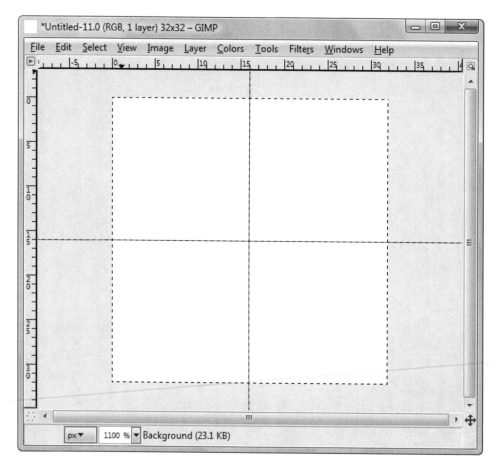

Figure 7.37
Guides to help us position our drawing.

Change the Foreground color using the settings like those seen in Figure 7.39. This is a shade of blue, but if you prefer, you can create red or any color you would like for your game.

Next, use the Bucket Fill tool and fill the ellipse. Your image should look something like Figure 7.40.

We're going to use the Ellipse Select tool again, but this time to create a smaller ellipse inside of the larger ellipse, as shown in Figure 7.41. The smaller ellipse will make up a "cockpit" area of the ship. Fill the smaller ellipse from our earlier blue shade to white using the Blend tool, as shown in Figure 7.42.

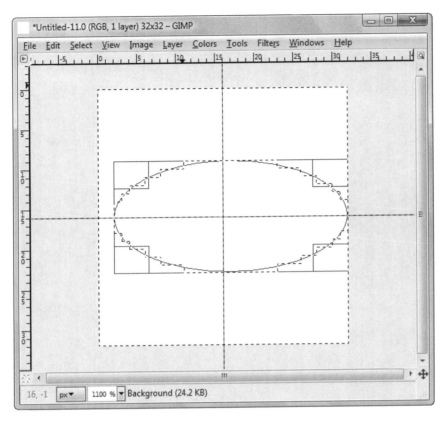

Figure 7.38
An ellipse is a good shape for the body of our ship.

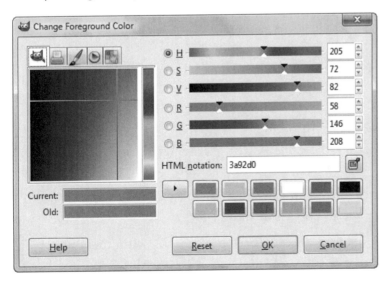

Figure 7.39
A basic color for our ship.

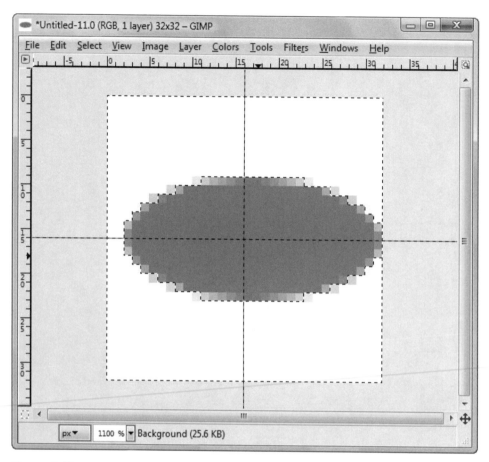

Figure 7.40
Filling the ellipse.

Next, use the Paintbrush tool and the smallest brush size you can find in the Brushes Toolbox to paint around the edge with a darker gray color, as shown in Figure 7.43.

We can now add some features such as an exhaust area. To do this, we will use the Free Select tool to draw a triangle as shown in Figure 7.44.

Using a darker shade of the earlier blue color, you can fill with the Bucket Fill tool. Once filled, your image will look like Figure 7.45. Next, using the Eraser tool, remove some of the image, as shown in Figure 7.46, to create a separation

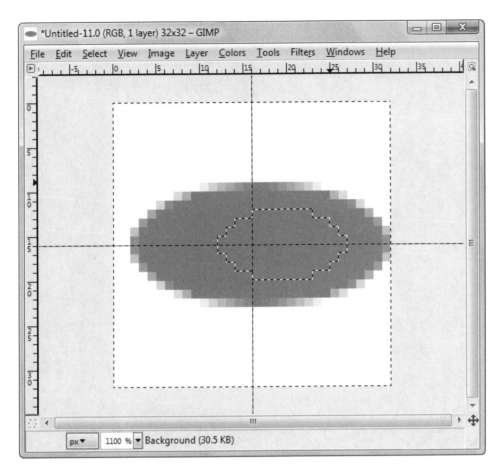

Figure 7.41
The color needs to be set as follows.

from the two exhaust areas. The next step is to draw a line using the Paintbrush tool. (Refer to Figure 7.47 for the location and thickness of the line.) Then click on a Selection tool to remove the current triangle selection and repeat drawing the line on the front of the ship, which is shown completed in Figure 7.48. The final step is to add "wings" to the side of the ship manually using the Paint Brush as shown in Figure 7.49.

To finish, drag the guides back to the rulers and zoom out to 100% to see if your efforts have paid off. You should be left with an image like the one shown in Figure 7.50.

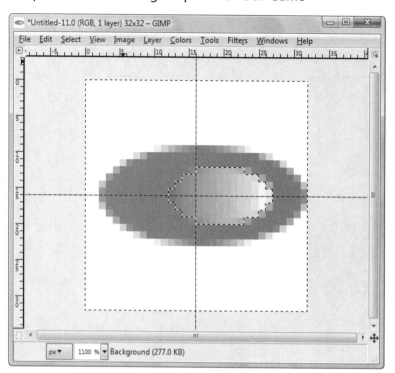

Figure 7.42
The Blend tool used in the smaller ellipse.

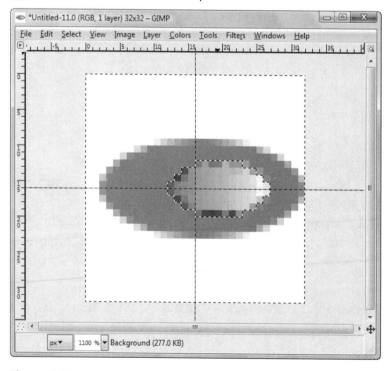

Figure 7.43
Adding a darker edge around the cockpit.

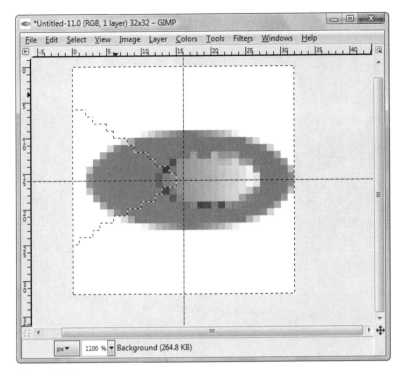

Figure 7.44
Draw a triangle with the help of the guides.

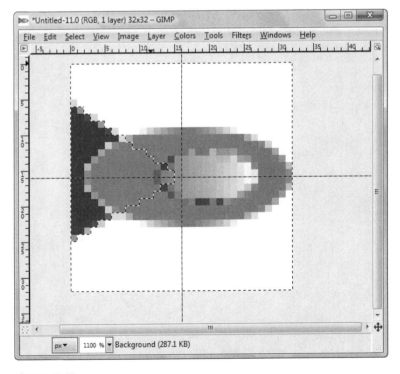

Figure 7.45
We have filled the area.

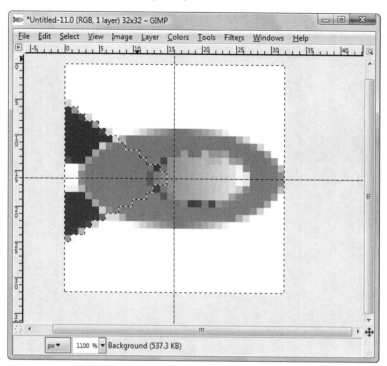

Figure 7.46
Create a separation of the exhaust.

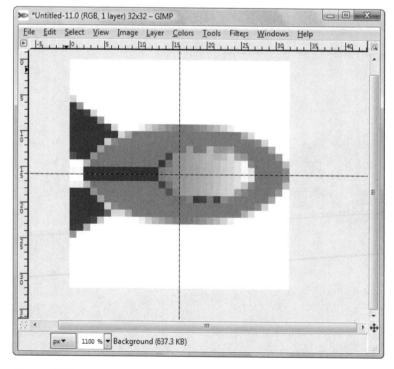

Figure 7.47
A line drawn on the back of the ship.

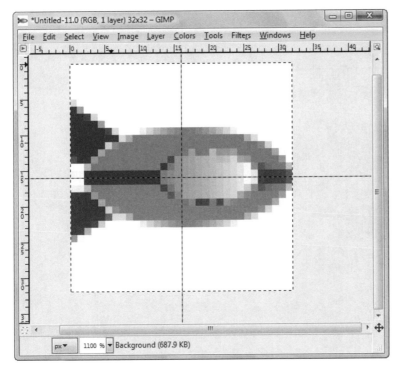

Figure 7.48
The line is drawn the full length of the ship.

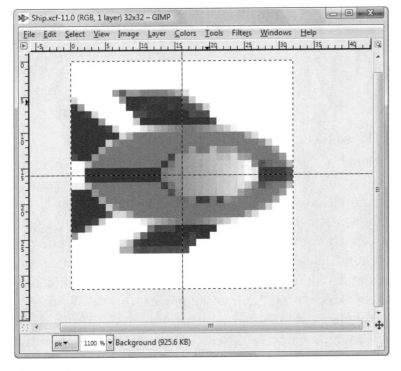

Figure 7.49
Wings added to the ship.

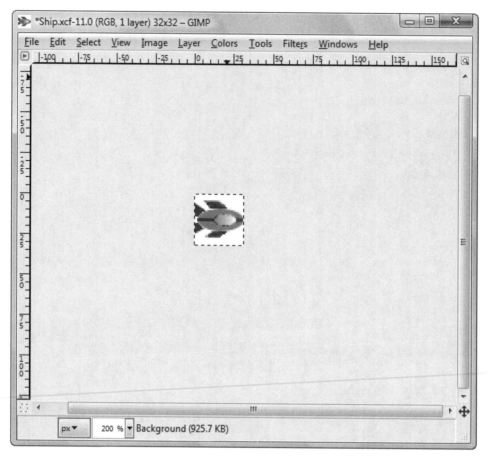

Figure 7.50
The final "hero" ship.

ASTEROIDS, LASERS, AND EXHAUST

Our game needs some additional items such as enemies, asteroids, lasers to shoot our enemies, and an exhaust for the ship when it's moving. We've already made a planet/moon earlier in the example, and you can use that as a guide to create the asteroids. The laser is simply a 6 × 6 image that has a line drawn through it to look like Figure 7.51. You can choose whatever colors you would like, but our example uses a shade of yellow. Likewise, the ship's exhaust is easy to create, again at 6 × 6 but using reds and yellow with the Paintbrush tool to create a simple image like Figure 7.52. Don't worry about animating it; we'll do that in another piece of software later. For the enemy ship, you can change the basic shape or just create another ship with a different color or several with different shapes and

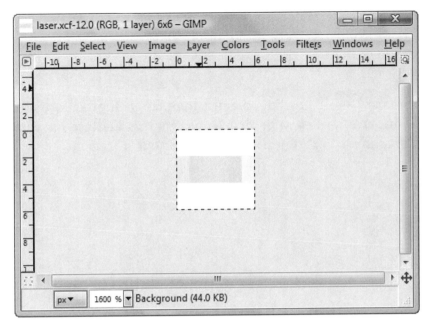

Figure 7.51
The laser is a 6 × 6 image with a line drawn through it.

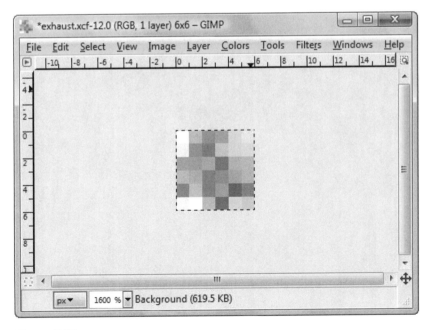

Figure 7.52
Creating the ship's exhaust.

colors. It's up to you and your imagination, and with what you have learned already, you have the set of skills necessary to do all of this and much more.

CHAPTER REVIEW

This has been the longest and most grueling chapter thus far in the book, but if you've followed along, you have created your first game graphics and are on your way to accomplishing the ultimate goal of learning to create your own game.

CHAPTER 8

CREATING MUSIC AND SOUND EFFECTS

Of the many components that go into making a video game, perhaps none are given less attention than sound effects and music. The addition of quality music and sound effects are one of the best ways to add production value to your games, but they are often overlooked. With believable sound effects and music, the player's emotional experience will be greatly enhanced and oftentimes it can make the difference between a good game and a great game.

MUSIC IN GAMES

As mentioned in Chapter 1, there are many parallels between making a movie and the development of a game. Hollywood has long realized the benefits of music and sound effects for the movie-watching experience. Over the past decade, tremendous time and resources have been spent on improving these aspects of a movie, during which time we have seen the increased use of surround sound in both theatrical and home movie releases.

The long and varied history of the movie industry offers us a tremendous amount of guidance. While you will find very little documentation on the creation of music and sound effects for games, there is a plethora of information available for the movie-maker, both professional and amateur. Countless books have been written and vast resources are available at websites, not to mention the movies themselves, which can often provide inspiration and ideas.

Beginning with the 42nd Annual Grammy Awards, the video game industry has started to receive recognition for its work. The NARAS (National Academy of

Recording Arts and Sciences) approved three new categories to include music written for "Other Visual Media." This includes the music from games—another example of the importance of music in your productions.

Basic Concepts

When you are given the assignment to create music for a game, you usually begin with a basic understanding of the type of music being requested. For instance, if you are creating music for a basketball game, classical music is probably not going to be appropriate. Your research often begins with discussing the piece or watching a specific type of program. Using the basketball example, you might watch a game on television or perhaps attend a game. This would give you a good idea of what the fans would experience.

On the other hand, if you were writing music for a game that reenacted the Civil War, you might watch movies or even talk with music historians about the types of instruments or music that were popular in the time period.

It's important to understand that you don't do this research so that you can simply copy the music. Instead, use this approach to discover what music fits the time, era, or genre and go from there. Like the graphics you create, music is an art form.

We're going to use ACID, a program we looked at previously in the book. This program offers several advantages over other applications. First, even if you don't have a music background, you can use ACID. Additionally, it comes with several samples that can be used in many ways. There are also several websites that have clips readily available for download to use with the program.

ACID Loops

ACID is based on the ability to create music from loops, much like most of the mainstream music being produced today. In the past 15–20 years, the vast majority of the music industry has utilized loops or samples in one aspect or another. This concept has drastically altered the music landscape, changing the way both amateur and professional producers create music. A quick listen of many modern albums will disclose the use of samples.

The use of samples in many forms of music has brought about an entire industry that produces music especially for this purpose. There are literally thousands of subscription websites and CDs that contain materials that can be used for almost any purpose. Along with the music that is available in standard audio formats like MP3 and WAV, there are also those that have been built with the file formats used by many leading music programs including ACID.

This data is distributed in two ways. There is a royalty-based system in which you are required to pay every time the sample is used. In fact, sometimes you can download the samples for free, but you pay as you use them. The other option usually involves paying a fee up front, but you then receive a royalty-free license that allows you to do most anything with the loops. With either option, you usually cannot distribute the material as a new collection of loops. Always follow the licensing agreements and pay careful attention to the details.

More recently, the Internet has offered a third and easier solution for obtaining samples. There are countless sites that offer fee-based downloads, whereas others allow you to download their loops freely. Sony's own ACIDPlanet.com offers free loops. It offers a freely available download every week called an 8Pack, which is essentially an ACID project file that includes eight loops, arranged into a song. The 8Packs will not only teach you how to combine loops into final projects, but it also comes with tips and tricks that were used to put it together.

CREATING YOUR MUSIC

Before we proceed, it's worth repeating a warning about loops. You need to thoroughly read the licensing agreement before downloading anything from a website or CD. To begin our composition, you should first register and download some loops from the ACIDPlanet.com website. I'm not going to encourage you to duplicate this project exactly, as the files that were downloaded may no longer exist. Simply download what is available right now to create a compilation. It isn't so important how our music sounds in this project. It's more important for you to understand its concepts so that you can make production-quality music for your later games.

When you open ACID, you'll be presented with an empty project, as shown in Figure 8.1.

Next, from the File menu choose Properties and set the information for your project, such as the title of the project and the copyright information. The New Project properties window can be seen in Figure 8.2.

Next, add your first loop to the project. Locate the file you downloaded and extracted from ACIDPlanet.com in the Explorer Window and double-click or drag it to the Track List to add it to your ACID project. If you want additional options, you can right-click and drag a file to the Track View or Track List to

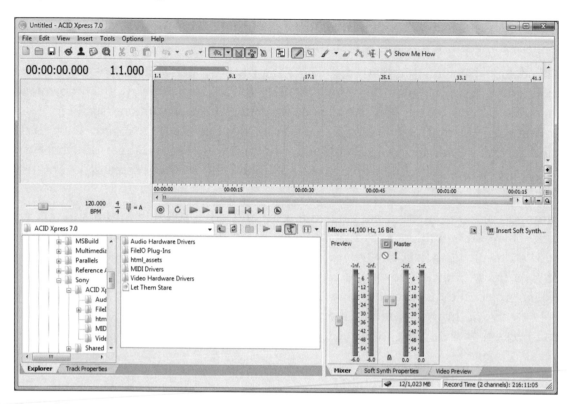

Figure 8.1
A new blank project in ACID.

Figure 8.2
The New Project properties window.

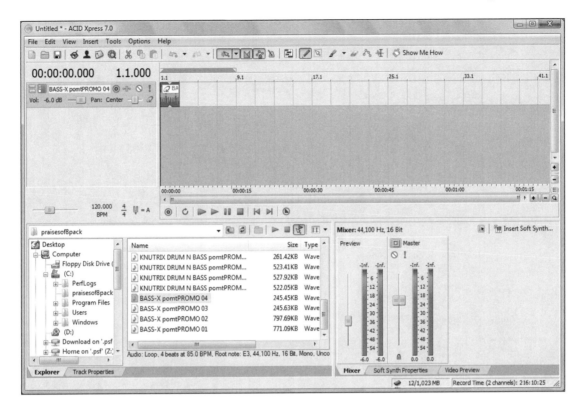

Figure 8.3
The project with a single loop added to it.

specify the type of track that will be created. A shortcut menu is displayed that allows you to choose whether the file will be treated as a loop, one-shot, Beat-mapped track, or as an autodetected type. Your project should look something like Figure 8.3. For now, you can use autodetect, but later you should read up on all of the options including the differences between Beatmapped tracks, loops, and one-shots. These definitions can get quite complicated, but you can read the help file to learn more about each.

Next, click and drag the time so that it ends at approximately 20 seconds. Your screen should now look like Figure 8.4. If for some reason your ruler has a different measure of time, you can change it by choosing View > Time Ruler and then selecting the appropriate format.

Next, you should select the Paint tool, which is designed to paint events across multiple tracks. With the Paint tool selected, you can paint events across multiple

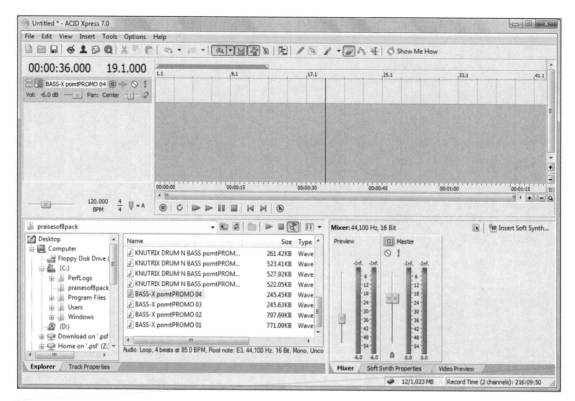

Figure 8.4
The audio is approximately 20 seconds.

tracks by clicking and dragging the mouse. This tool is also useful for inserting one-shot events evenly along the grid, which is basically how we are planning to use it.

With the Paint tool, draw in the first location in the grid directly to the right of the filename that can be seen in the Track List. Your project should look like Figure 8.5.

You can click the Play button to test the project before moving on. If it plays correctly, it would be a good time to save and give your project the name "MyFirstACIDProject."

The next step is to add the rest of your loops to the project. Once you have finished, you can begin creating your music by drawing with the Paint tool or Draw tool inside the grid next to the individual tracks. For an example, see Figure 8.6 to see the finished project.

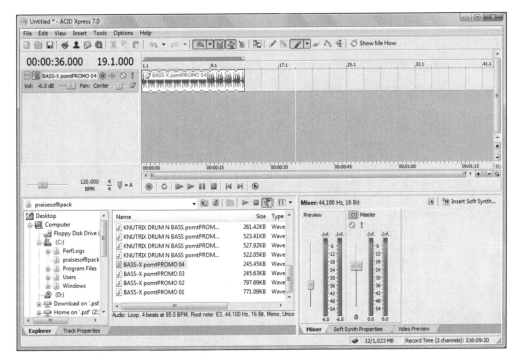

Figure 8.5
The first entry in the grid.

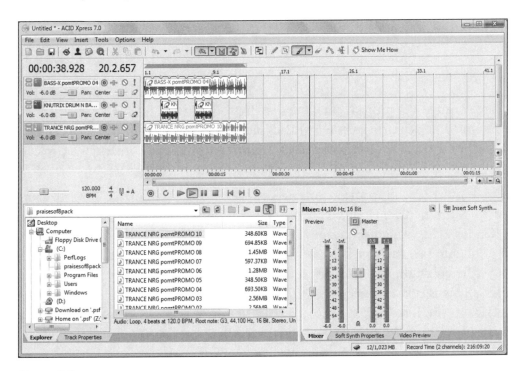

Figure 8.6
The finished project.

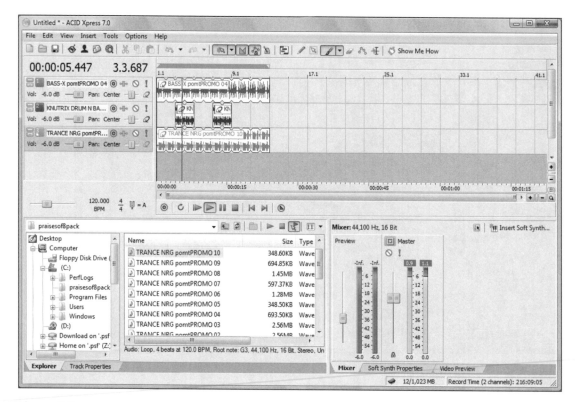

Figure 8.7
Playback of the project.

Once you have created the project, click the Play button to listen to it (Figure 8.7). You should take some time acquiring as many 8Packs as you can or purchasing packs so that you have a big library of loops to choose from. Acid Planet has pre-constructed projects that will give you an idea of how to put things together.

Once you have finished your project, you need to save it in MP3 format for our game to be used in Multimedia Fusion. You can do this by clicking the File menu and choosing Render. This will display the Render dialog, similar to the one shown in Figure 8.8. Fill out the various fields as shown in Figure 8.9 and click Save. You need to pay particular attention to the sound quality settings, as they are limited in ACID Xpress. This is not a problem for this project, but if you get to the point where you would like to produce higher quality music, you can upgrade to the Pro version. Now that we have some music, we can turn our attention to the creation of sound effects.

Figure 8.8
The Render window in ACID.

Figure 8.9
Settings for our project.

CREATING SOUND EFFECTS

Sound is everywhere in our daily life so it's obvious why it would be so important to a game player. Sound effects often take on meaning in a game. A dark battlefield with explosions in the background delivers a message of fear more than the field would by itself in silence. Soldiers yelling loudly might draw our attention to an area or might make us want to run in the opposite direction depending on what they are saying. You can also use sound effects to establish a time and a place. For instance, background noise such as a waterfall, rain, or even insects can add a great deal to a setting without visually changing anything.

Sound effects can also have far more obvious uses, such as to convey actions like a gun being fired or a car colliding with a wall in a racing game. It is this part of sound effects, the part that adds emotion or action to a scene, that game programmers are most interested. Like the loops we found for ACID, there are also sound effects libraries that can be purchased, and some are even open source or in the public domain. For the vast majority of sound effects, there are probably libraries that contain something that will work or can be modified slightly to work. It is this approach that most game developers take.

For those sounds that are unique or for sounds you'd just prefer to create yourself, it is often a very simple process. If you have your iPhone or a portable digital recorder of some sort, you can often visit a site to obtain sound recordings. For instance, if you have a game with animals, a visit to a local zoo is often all you would need to add the appropriate noises. If you are creating a sports title, visiting a local sporting event will give you all of the crowd and background noises you would ever need.

If you choose to visit local areas to record your noises, keep in mind that you'll often need more than you would have imagined. Poor sound quality could leave you with only minutes from a 10-minute recorded segment after editing. Again, you should always try to get more material than you think you'll need.

The other basic type of sound effect for a game occurs when some type of action happens. The action types take a great deal of time to produce and may require a tremendous amount of specialized equipment. Fortunately, with a little effort and common items, you can use some very simple ideas to record these types of sound for our game.

Recording Sounds

It doesn't really matter what type of device you use to record the sounds. Ultimately, you will have to get the data into the computer. The first step in this process is downloading samples or creating the recordings. We're going to create a basic space shooter, and with this in mind, we'll need to create effects for a variety of items. Rather than start from scratch, we'll use some pre-made options available from www.pdsounds.com or www.soundbible.com and then edit them. We'll do this in the next section, but to help you along with the thought process, we'll take a look at some ways you can create your own effects rather simply at home.

Manufacturing Sounds

If you are so inclined, creating and recording sound effects is not too difficult. The following list describes several types of actions that you can record easily with common household items. We aren't actually using any of these for our project, but it's helpful to see how simple it is to create the sounds you need.

- **Car Crash.** To create a crash, you can use a cardboard box with scrap metal and chunks of wood inside. Shaking it with different levels of intensity will allow you to get a variety of sounds in your recording.

- **Fire.** Take a piece of cellophane positioned a distance from the recording device and slowly crinkle it with your hands.

- **Door Slamming.** You can use a real door and simply place the recording device near the hinges. You can slam the door and then open and close the door slowly if you also need a creaking door type of noise.

- **Body Collisions.** To simulate someone being punched or a collision between bodies, you can strike a pumpkin or watermelon with a piece of wood or rubber mallet. Try various methods to get just the right sound but be careful; this is messy. Another method is to wrap wet towels around wood planks and then strike them together or let them fall a small distance to a concrete or hardwood surface.

- **Rain.** You can simply record rain on a roof or metal sheet, or if you are in a hurry, you can simulate the effect by taping together five plastic cups having cut the bottoms of the cups into different shapes such as a square, star, or ellipse. After taping them together, you can poor uncooked rice into the top and as it falls through, it will sound like rain falling.

- **Thunder.** Thunder can be recorded during a storm, but like rain, it can be simulated using other methods. You can create a simple "thunder sheet" by getting a piece of sheet metal cut approximately 18" × 50". Then fit with 1" × 2" boards on one end and multiple holes in the other to hang it from a ceiling or beam. You can shake the end with the handle to simulate the thunder. This can take some practice to master, so be patient if it doesn't sound realistic at first.

■ **Footsteps.** Depending on your needs, it is probably easiest to emulate footsteps by recording the real thing. You can record in gravel areas for outdoor simulations or you could use a hardwood floor with hard-heeled shoes for indoor areas. If you would prefer, you can actually construct a wooden box large enough to step into. It would need to be approximately 3′ × 3′ and once constructed, you can step in place. This helps to amplify the sounds so that they are easier to record. Additionally, you can flip it over for recording step noises or you can fill it with things like straw or newspaper to vary the noises so they sound like leaves crunching as you walk. To simulate walking in snow, you can use a shoe to press on an old couch cushion or similar type of furniture. If you do this at the approximate stepping rhythm, it will simulate this very well. You can also simulate animal footsteps using similar methods. For instance, you can simulate a horse by striking small squares of wood together or by striking together halves of a coconut with all of the pulp removed. You could use your box along with the coconut by adding some kitty litter or sand and then striking the halves with the box. This will emulate the sound of an animal moving through a sandy terrain.

■ **Machines.** You should try to record the actual machine noises. For instance, if you are creating a car racing game, you might get the best effects by visiting a race and recording the sounds yourself. Additional sounds that work well in games include tools like saws, drills, and even hammers.

■ **Gunshots.** Hitting a leather seat with a thin wooden stick such as a yardstick or ruler can simulate gunshots. For different types of sounds, you can experiment by hitting other materials with the wooden stick.

■ **Gun Shots Breaking Wood.** You can cut plywood into thin strips and then break them while recording. It will sound as if the shots are splintering the wood.

■ **Aircraft/Spacecraft.** Visit an airport and record the different airplanes taking off and landing. You can edit these files later in Audacity to make them more suitable for your needs.

Creating these types of sound effects is very much trial and error. As such, you should spend some time finding several objects that sound good and record all of them. You can follow this same basic process for creating the other sound effects using the methods we looked at previously in the chapter.

Creating a Flying Spaceship Sound Effect

With some basic concepts in place, let's use Audacity to create a sound effect for our spaceship when it is thrusting. To begin, download from SoundBible.com a file called Spitfire or any type of machine noise that you would like to use as a basis for this project. Again, it's worth noting that the licensing of files is important so always make sure you can use the files in your projects.

Once you download the file, open Audacity. Next, from the File menu choose Open and locate the file that you downloaded. It should look something like Figure 8.10.

You can listen to the sound effect using the playback controls in Audacity. Listen to the file several times. We are only really interested in a few seconds of sound that we want to keep, so take some time to find an area that sounds interesting. Using the selection tools, select an area (Figure 8.11) and then choose Copy from the Edit menu.

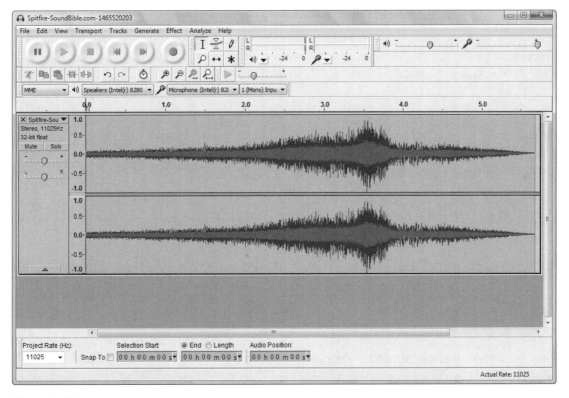

Figure 8.10
The basic sound opened in Audacity.

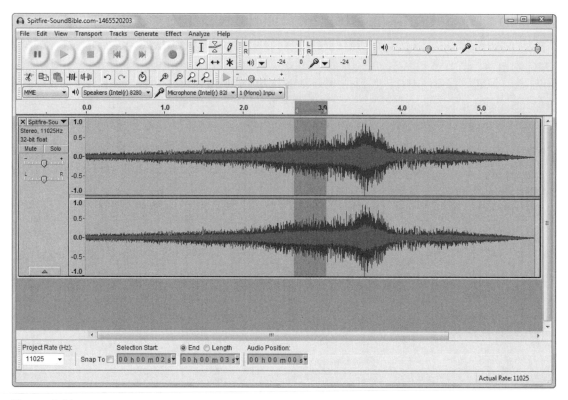

Figure 8.11
Select a small sample of sound.

Next, create a new blank file by choosing File > New. Inside this new window in Audacity, we'll use Edit > Paste to add our content that was previously selected. You can see this pasted into a new project in Figure 8.12.

Now, take a moment to play it back so that you can make sure this is the basic sound you are after. If not, close the file, select a different sample from the initial sound effect and then paste again until you get something that you like.

If you are happy with the file, let's change it into something slightly different so that it better reflects a flying spaceship.

You can use Generate > Noise as a quick effect. You can see the menu option in Figure 8.13.

Play the sound back again to make sure you like it. If not, you can choose Undo from the Edit menu and be back to the original file. Next, you can use the Envelope tool to change the sound again. The Envelope tool has been selected in Figure 8.14.

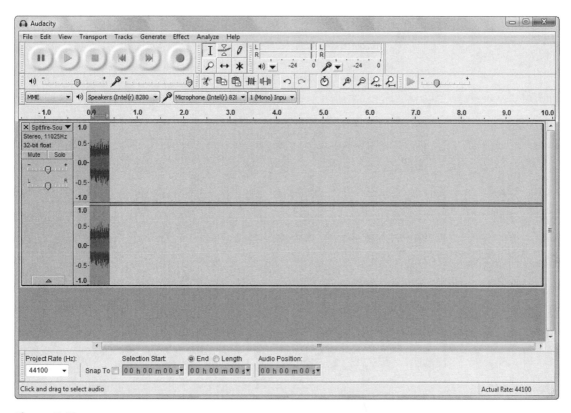

Figure 8.12
Our audio in a new project by itself.

Figure 8.13
Adding noise to the sound.

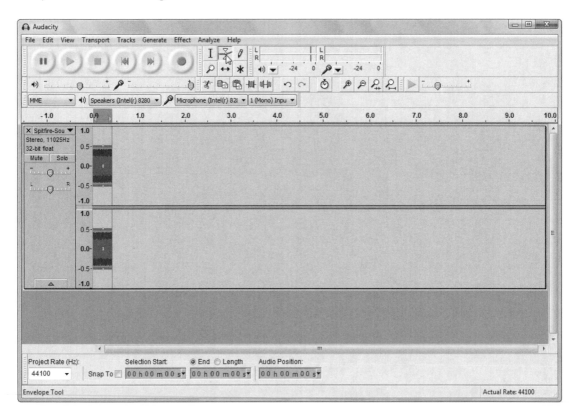

Figure 8.14
Using the Envelope tool.

It's sounding close to what we need, but we can continue to tweak it. Let's increase the Playback Speed to make a small but noticeable difference in the sound. You can play with various speeds, but Figure 8.15 displays some figures that worked well on this sample.

Play it back again and see how it sounds. If it's good, we need to increase the sound so that it's a bit longer. You can simply select the entire track length; choose Copy and then Paste from the Edit menu to add it to the project. You can now use the Time Shift tool to place it directly to the right of the original sample, which you can see in Figure 8.16. We now have a duplicate of our original sound, making this sample twice the size. Play it back, and if you are happy, save the file in MP3 format and you are finished. If it needs to be longer, use Copy and Paste to increase the length of the sound or further edit using Audacity's tools.

Using these same basic principles and methods, you can create sound effects for the entire game, such as explosions and even lasers shooting in space.

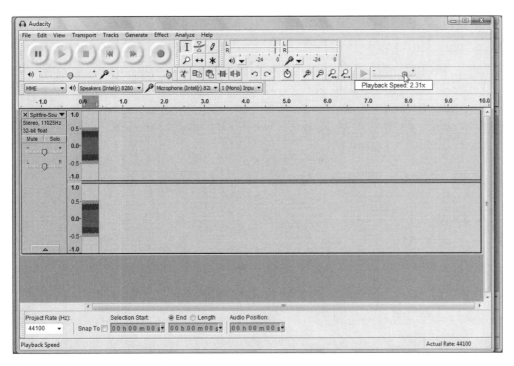

Figure 8.15
Adjusting the speed of playback can quickly change the sound.

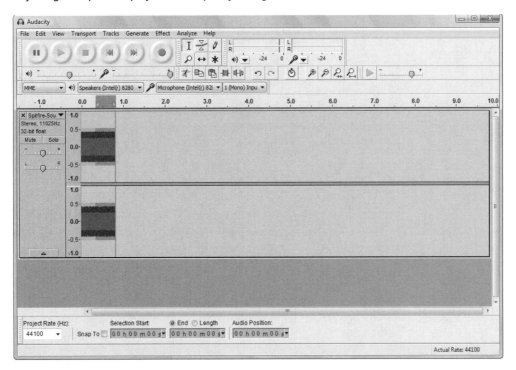

Figure 8.16
Increasing the length of the sound.

CHAPTER REVIEW

It's easy to see why music and sound effects are so important to the development of a game. They can add so much to the experience by setting a mood or even identifying a location. Well-thought-out music and sound effects go hand in hand with the eye candy that so many developers focus on. It has become an integral part of the game development process. In the next chapter, we'll turn our attention to Multimedia Fusion and start building a game.

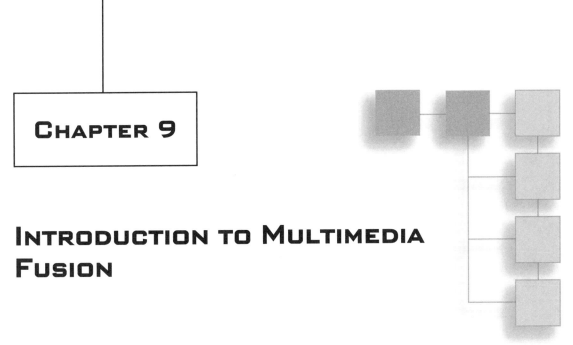

CHAPTER 9

INTRODUCTION TO MULTIMEDIA FUSION

In this chapter, we are going to create our first game using an application called Multimedia Fusion. We'll use the full name of Multimedia Fusion and MMF interchangeably throughout the book. This development tool is mostly used for 2D games, but because it is the most well-rounded game development tool available that can create games for multiple genres, it's a perfect way to start out. With it, you can create a wide variety of games for many platforms (iPhone, Android, Windows, Mac, Xbox using XNA) and the support from Clickteam (www.clickteam.com) and the users on the Clickteam forums is fantastic. You will need to purchase the exporters for the various platforms from Clickteam if you decide to make games for platforms besides Windows.

INSTALLING MULTIMEDIA FUSION AND EXTENSIONS

Before we can use Multimedia Fusion, we must first install it. The installation process begins by downloading the most up-to-date version from the Clickteam website, or you can find links on my website (www.claytoncrooks.com). Once you have the file, double-click it to open it, which will display something like Figure 9.1.

Click the Next button on the first screen, which brings us to the second window (Figure 9.2) of our installation. This screen will display a quick overview of the installation process we are now going through. You need to accept the terms of

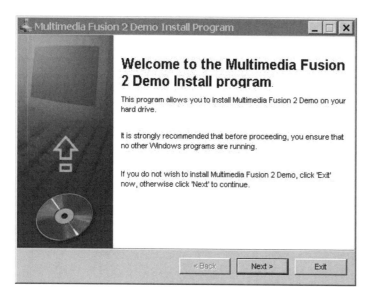

Figure 9.1
The opening screen for the installation.

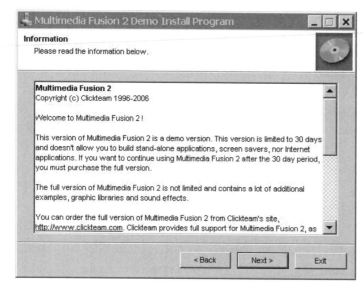

Figure 9.2
An overview of the installation process.

the installation agreement after reading through it. License agreements are placed their by the developer and the legalities of them are far beyond the scope of this book. You will need to click that you agree to the terms before you can proceed, as you can see in Figure 9.3, and then click Next.

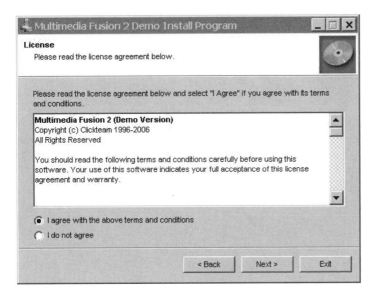

Figure 9.3
You need to accept the terms.

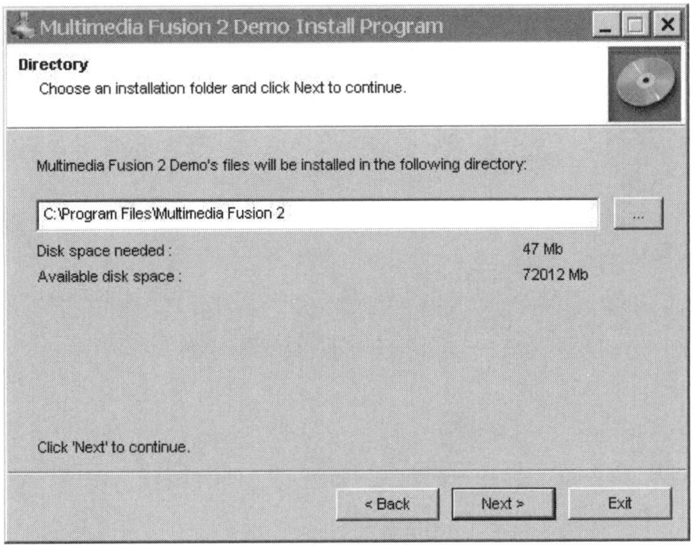

Figure 9.4
Check on the location before clicking Next.

The next window displays a location for the install (Figure 9.4). This screen allows you to verify the location where the files will be stored. Verify this and then click Next. You will see a new window that looks something like Figure 9.5. Click Start and the files will extract, as shown in Figure 9.6, and finally you will see the end of the install. Click Exit.

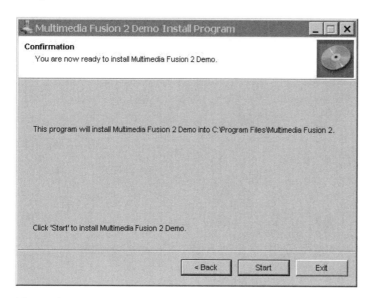

Figure 9.5
Last step before file extraction.

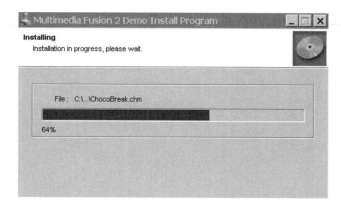

Figure 9.6
Installation files are being extracted.

Multimedia Fusion Interface

In the next few chapters, we are going to build our first games step by step. Much of what you learn here will apply to more complex games and tools later on. You will find it easier to learn new software and tools after studying this application.

We'll now take the time to learn MMF's interface. Once you are comfortable with MMF, you will be able to use it to produce games and interactive applications with ease. MMF is a very powerful 2D/3D game creation package. It contains state-of-the-art animation tools, sound tools, multimedia functions, and fabulous game structuring routines that make it very easy to produce your own games all with no programming.

Quick Guide to MMF Editors

MMF is built around three main editing screens that allow you to control the primary aspects of your game. The Storyboard Editor is the screen that allows you to decide the order of the levels in the game. The Level Editor allows you to decide which characters, backgrounds, and objects to put in your level and how to animate them. The Event Editor allows you to assign the actions and responses that will make your game come alive.

Let's start MMF and take a look at some of these windows. When you first open MMF from the shortcuts that were created during the installation, a window will appear, reminding you that it is the demo version (Figure 9.7). You can click Continue after reading through this information. The main interface of MMF now appears (Figure 9.8).

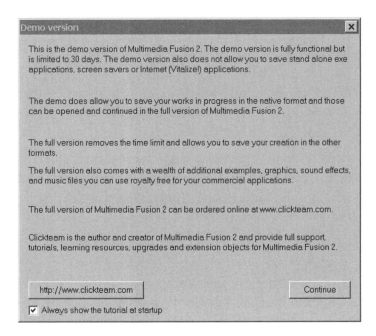

Figure 9.7
Demo information is displayed on startup.

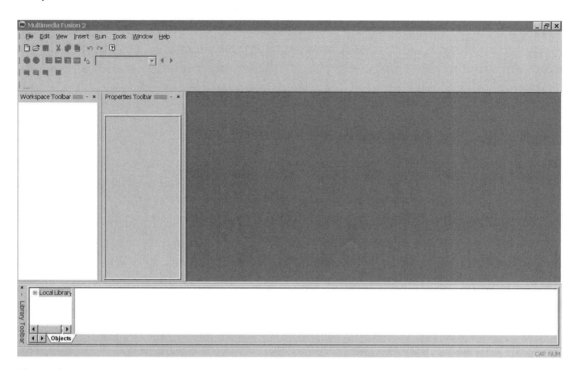

Figure 9.8
The MMF Interface is displayed.

As you can see along the bottom left side, a smaller window is visible, which is called the Multimedia Fusion Library window. You can close this window by clicking the small X at its upper right. We prefer to open this window only if needed rather than allowing it to consume so much of our free space all the time. Figure 9.9 represents the much larger space that we now have to work with.

Click New from the File menu to create your first game. Once you have created the new file, click on Application, which is displayed in Figure 9.10. You will see several options for creating the application. Choose Stand-Alone Application from the Build Type Drop-Down List.

Our MMF interface has now changed dramatically (see Figure 9.11). On the right is the Storyboard Editor, which displays an overview of our application in the form of a thumbnail and also allows you to quickly access every frame our games use. Let's take a more in-depth look at this and some of the editors we are going to use. The following descriptions should give you a better understanding of the editor screens and you can refer to the help file included with MMF if you would like additional information.

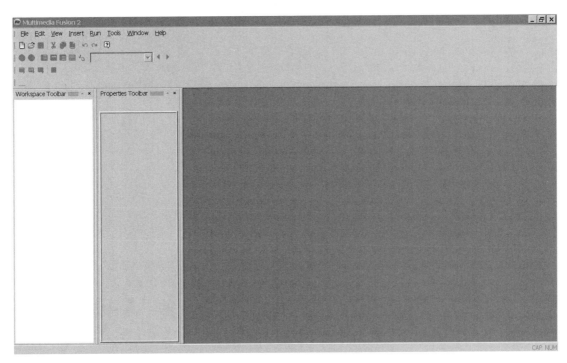

Figure 9.9
We have gained a considerable amount of space by closing the window.

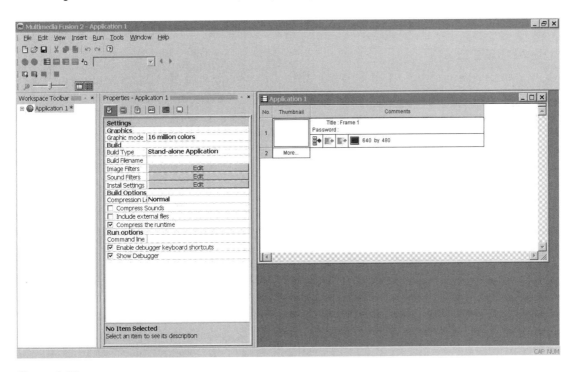

Figure 9.10
Creating a new application.

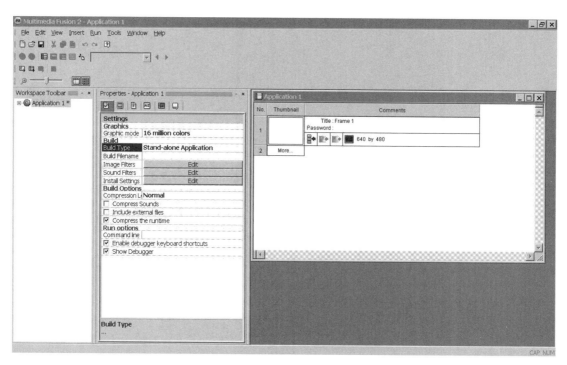

Figure 9.11
The interface has changed.

Storyboard Editor

Most games are composed of several different levels, and this screen allows you to add levels to your game, copy levels, and change the order of the levels by moving them around. This is also where you decide on the size of your playing area, add and edit professional-looking fades to each level, and assign passwords to enter a level if you would like. (See Figure 9.12.)

Frame Editor

The Frame Editor (Figure 9.13) is the initial "blank page" for each of your levels. It displays your play area and is where you put background objects and the main characters of your game. You generally access this screen from the Storyboard Editor screen.

This is also where you can create your own animated objects, text, and other object types. Basically, all the objects that you want to play with have to be placed on this screen first before you can start manipulating them. It is also here that you change the animation and movement of objects, and change the basic setup of all your

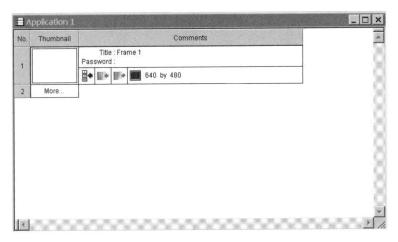

Figure 9.12
The Storyboard Editor.

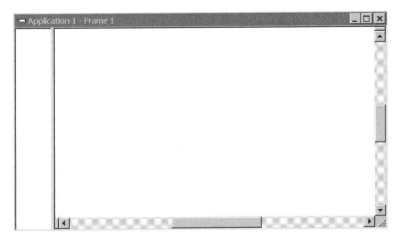

Figure 9.13
The Frame Editor.

objects. You will frequently find that before you can manipulate an object from the Event Editor, you must make sure that it is set up correctly on this screen.

Event Editor

This is where your game will really come to life. The actions you assign here are called interactivity. Once you become experienced with MMF, you will find that this editor is where you will spend most of your time. It is here that you decide all the events in your game.

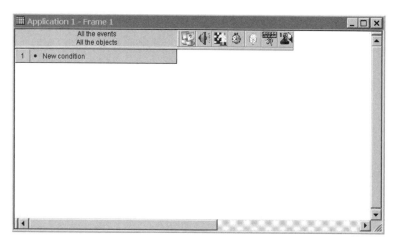

Figure 9.14
The Event Editor.

The Event Editor (see Figure 9.14) is set up like a spreadsheet, where you can assign relationships to each object in your game. This setup makes game-building much easier as you can see what happens in your game as you build it. Examples of the game play you can build are aliens colliding with a spaceship; the main character collecting a power-up or getting hit by a missile; setting a time limit; or assigning a sound event. You can create an explosion, destroy an object, add to the score, subtract a life, or even add complicated events like changing the direction of a character or randomly moving object.

That was a quick tour of MMF and the main editors. We saw that a game is built in MMF in three stages: First, you lay out the flow of your game in the Storyboard Editor, then you lay out your level and its objects in the Frame Editor, and finally you use the Event Editor to assign relationships and behaviors to your objects.

CHAPTER REVIEW

In this chapter, we looked at Multimedia Fusion and covered the installation of the basic tool. We also introduced the user interface of MMF and its main editors. In the next couple of chapters, we will build a simple game to get started learning about the power of MMF and will then build our final game for the iPhone.

CHAPTER 10

OUR FIRST GAME IN MMF

Now that we have a foundation in MMF, and can understand its layout and editors, we can move on to building our first game. This project will be a great foundation for other games as we'll try to cover a variety of topics that you can use again and again in your future work.

LET'S GET STARTED

The first step in building our game project is to open MMF. Once open, from the File menu choose New. This will open a window that allows us to create a new game. Click on Application, or if you have already installed the iOS exporter, you can choose an XCode project with 480 × 320 settings from the window and click OK. You now see many of the editors that we spent time looking at in the last chapter.

Note

A frame and level are actually the same basic concepts in MMF and are used interchangeably. Most often, a level refers to the game play aspect whereas a frame refers to the game design.

The numbers along the left of the Storyboard Editor indicate the various levels that are available in our game. At this time, we have only a single level, which was created for us automatically when we created the project. We can open this by clicking on the number 1. This will open the Frame Editor for our first level. You can see this in Figure 10.1.

At this time, we have a blank level so we need to begin constructing the environment that will make up the game. From the View menu, choose Toolbars > Library Window (see Figure 10.2). This will display a window like Figure 10.3.

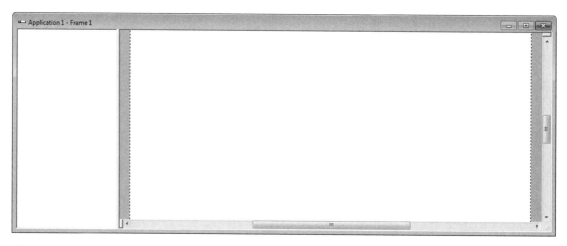

Figure 10.1
MMF's Storyboard Editor.

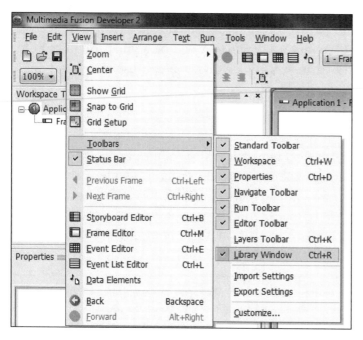

Figure 10.2
The Library Window menu.

Figure 10.3
MMF's Object Library.

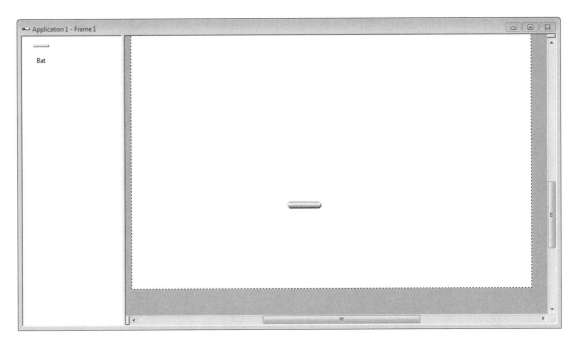

Figure 10.4
Our first frame with a "bat" object.

As you can see in Figure 10.3, there is a "+" symbol next to the "Local Library" folder. This "+" symbol can be clicked to open the folder. Continue to click the symbol until you see the Games folder displayed. Open this folder in the same manner and find the item called Game objects 2. Single-click the "bat" item and then drag it inside the frame that has been empty up to this point in time. You should now see the item in the frame, as shown in Figure 10.4.

You can now zoom out so that you can see the entire frame by choosing Zoom > Out from the View menu. Continue to zoom out on the frame until you can see the entire frame within the Frame Editor similar to Figure 10.5.

The reason we want to see the entire frame is so that we can place items more quickly within the frame as needed. We can position the bat by clicking it and dragging it so that it is similar to Figure 10.6.

The next two steps are to insert additional objects repeating the same steps as you did earlier with the bat. You need game objects for the ball and the bricks and can choose from the objects to pick the ones you like best. Figures 10.7 and 10.8 display the Ball1 and Brick1 objects in their respective positions.

You can save your project at this time. Feel free to save it with any name you would prefer by using the Save menu from the File menu.

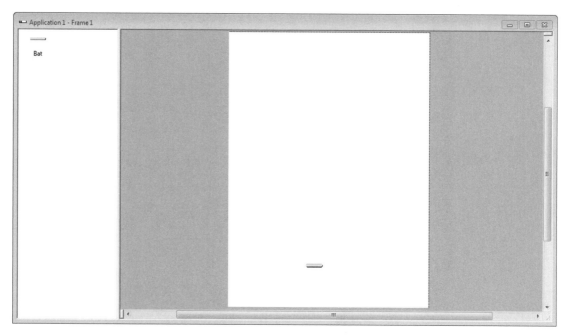

Figure 10.5
The frame should look similar to this.

Figure 10.6
You can position the "bat" using this as a reference.

Figure 10.7
The ball has been placed in the level.

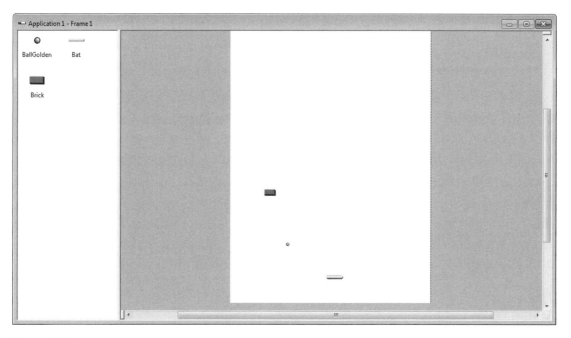

Figure 10.8
We need bricks to destroy.

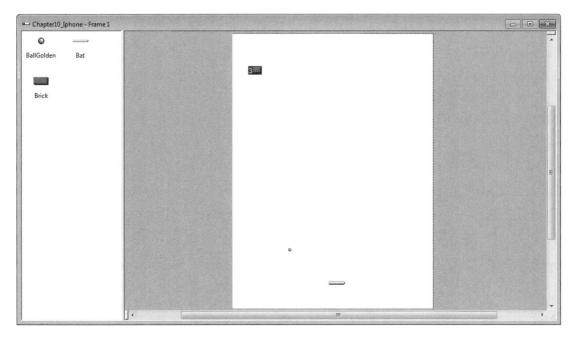

Figure 10.9
The brick placed at the upper left.

Note

Although MMF is very stable, it is a good habit to often save your work when developing games. We have done this as a reminder and you should continue doing so as you work through the examples in the book and on your own.

A single brick doesn't really make for much of a game. In fact, one collision between the brick and ball would end the game. With that in mind, we're going to duplicate the brick so that all of the original brick's properties will be given to the duplicates. We can then handle the collisions as if we had added a single item to our project. First, position a brick in the upper left like in Figure 10.9.

The next step is to right-click the brick and choose Duplicate from the pop-up menu. This will display the Duplicate Object window like the one shown in Figure 10.10. This window provides several options, which are all self-explanatory. You can use the following settings for this project and then click OK when finished:

Rows: 11

Columns: 9

Row Spacing: 5

Column Spacing: 5

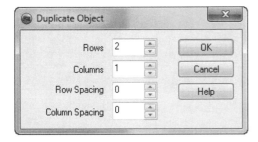

Figure 10.10
The Duplicate Object window.

MOVEMENT

Our level now looks like Figure 10.11. If we were to run the game at this time, we would be left with a screen of objects that don't really do anything. For any type of game project, we'll need to create movement of objects. Let's begin with the ball. Single-click on this object and then from the Properties window click the third icon that looks like a person moving (see Figure 10.12).

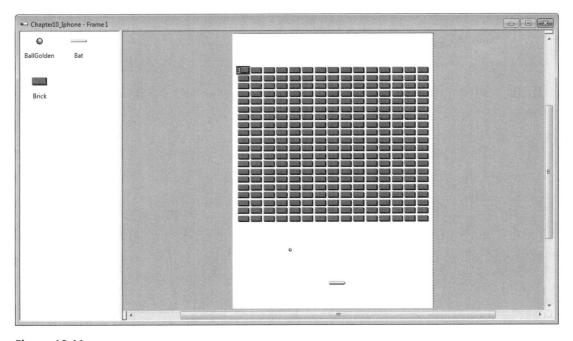

Figure 10.11
Your screen now looks like this.

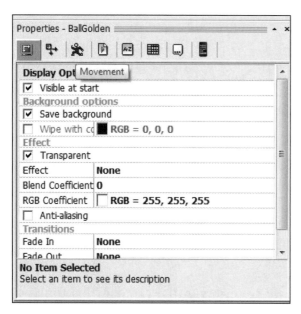

Figure 10.12
The first step in creating a new movement.

Figure 10.13
This window allows us to set up the type of movement for our object.

You should now have the Movement options on your screen (Figure 10.13). For this movement, there is a built-in option for a bouncing ball. Click the Static symbol to open the options (see Figure 10.14). Select the Ball Movement option, and you can simply leave these setting with their default values at this time and click the OK button to close it.

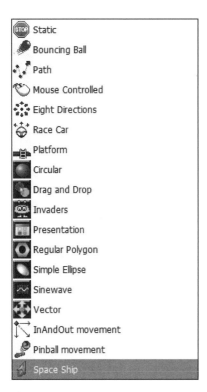

Figure 10.14
Ball Movement window has specific options for ball movements.

The ball now has movement, but the bat in our game is left without any. Single-click the bat and then choose Eight Directions from the Properties window. The Eight Directions movement screen is now displayed (see Figure 10.15).

Unlike the ball movement, which was fine with the default settings, we are going to need to change some of the options for this movement. Click the Directions button to open the window that looks like Figure 10.16. You can deselect all movements by clicking on the black squares so that left and right are the only directions selected. Your window now looks like Figure 10.17.

The next step is to click the Initial Direction button, which looks like the Directions options we were just looking at. We need to remove all direction options from this window and can do so by clicking each of them, or we can click the button in the lower right to deselect all of them simultaneously (see Figure 10.18). Press Enter or Return to close the settings.

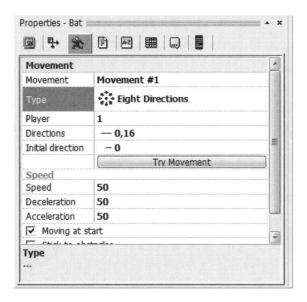

Figure 10.15
The Eight Direction movement screen.

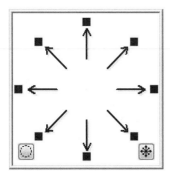

Figure 10.16
The Directions window showing the default options.

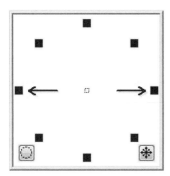

Figure 10.17
Left and right should be the only squares selected.

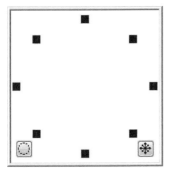

Figure 10.18
Deselect all directions.

MULTIMEDIA FUSION EVENTS

We now have a game that contains objects, and their movements have been set, but that's about it. Nothing will happen when the objects collide with one another. This would obviously limit any type of fun you'd have playing it. To set this up, we are going to need to open the Event Editor. There are several ways to open the Event Editor; you can click on its icon (Figure 10.19) or you can choose Event Editor from the View menu. Lastly, you can use the shortcut combination of CTRL + E to open it. You can use the method you prefer.

Once the window is open, click New Condition to display the New Condition window (Figure 10.20).

Double-click the Ball icon in the window. This will display the menu you can see in Figure 10.21. We are setting up the collision that will occur between the brick and the ball so we need to choose Collisions > Another Object. This will open the Test a Collision window shown in Figure 10.22. Choose Brick from the available objects and then click OK. Your Event Editor is now updated with this collision (see Figure 10.23).

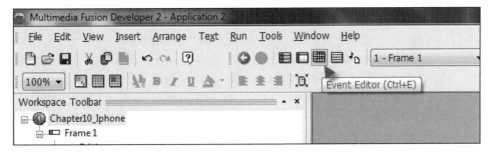

Figure 10.19
This icon is one way to open the editor.

Figure 10.20
The New Condition window.

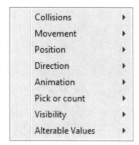

Figure 10.21
The menu options.

Now we have a collision event that will be executed every time a ball and brick collide. When the objects collide during the game, the Event Editor will cause an action to occur but we have yet to create the exact action we would like to have. At this time, we are going to right-click on the square beneath the column in which the brick is displayed (Figure 10.24). You can choose Destroy from the pop-up menu. A check mark is now visible inside the Event Editor within the intersection points of the action and the brick column like the one shown in Figure 10.25.

Now the bricks are going to be destroyed when a ball collides with them, but if the ball collides with the bat, it will simply continue through it. We need to make it

Figure 10.22
Test a Collision window.

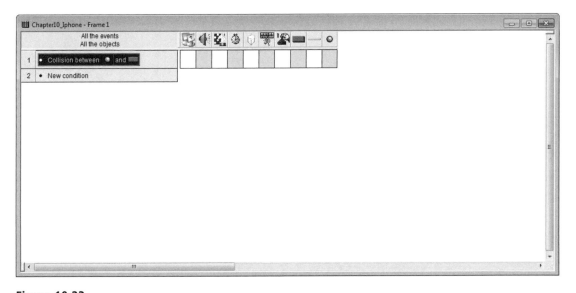

Figure 10.23
The event has been created.

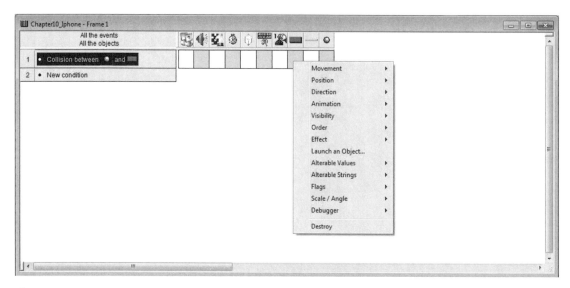

Figure 10.24
The brick column.

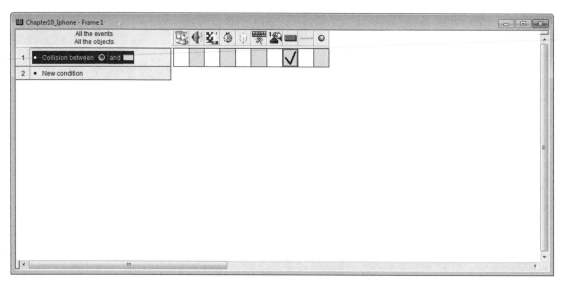

Figure 10.25
A check mark is now visible.

bounce during such a collision. We can create the event the same way we did for the brick and ball, but this time we need to substitute the bat (Figure 10.26).

We have the event and now need to create an action. As already mentioned, we would like the ball to bounce with this collision after the brick is destroyed. Right-click the square beneath the ball and then choose Movement > Bounce (Figure 10.27).

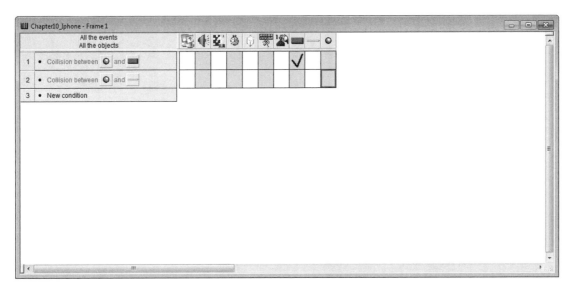

Figure 10.26
The brick is replaced by the bat in this event.

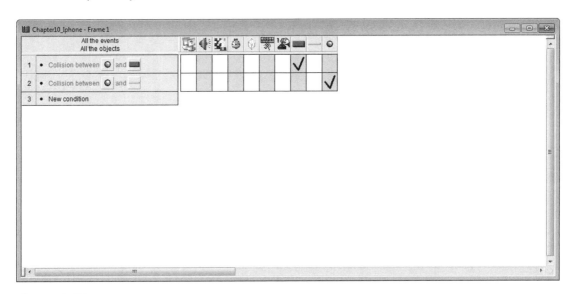

Figure 10.27
The ball will now bounce.

We now have the ball moving and colliding with the objects on the screen, but if the ball reaches any of the screen borders, it will continue to move into empty space never to be seen again. We will create an event to handle this as well.

First, click New Condition and then double-click Ball. Choose Position > Test position of "BallGolden" (or whatever ball you chose) as seen in Figure 10.28. The Test Position window is displayed (Figure 10.29). Click on the arrows inside of the square

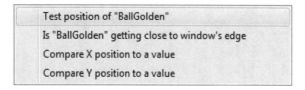

Figure 10.28
The pop-up menu has many options.

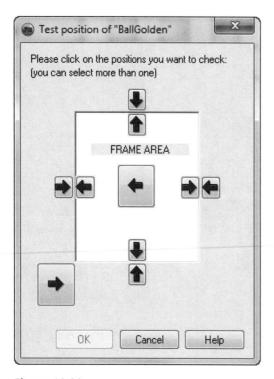

Figure 10.29
The Test Position of "BallGolden" window.

for left, right, and up but not down and click OK. The reason for this is simple. If the ball tries to leave in the screen on the left side, right ride, or top direction, we need to have the ball bounce. If it leaves the bottom, we need an entirely different approach. The new entry in the Event Editor is seen as ball leaves play area on top, left, or right (Figure 10.30). Right-click the column beneath Ball and choose Movement > Bounce.

The last event in this chapter again deals with the ball and testing its position, but this time, we need to create the event with the ball leaving the bottom position. Click on New Condition, and then double-click the ball from the window. Choose Position > Test Position. From the Test Position window, click the bottom arrow (Figure 10.31) and then click OK.

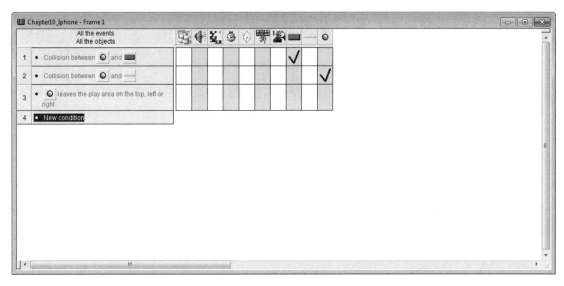

Figure 10.30
The new entry in the Event Editor.

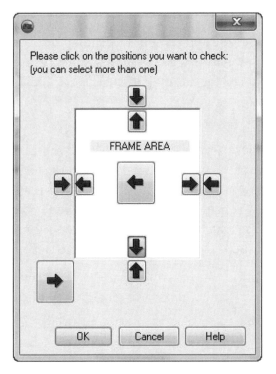

Figure 10.31
Choose the bottom arrow.

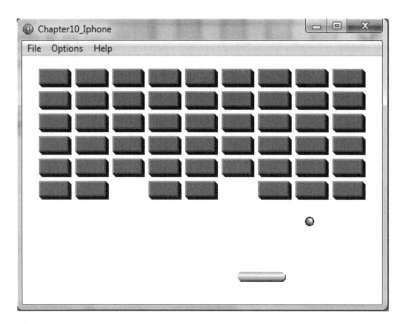

Figure 10.32
The game is running.

Right-click on the "chess board square" and choose End the Application. Save the game by choosing File > Save and then choose Play to try out the application. Depending on your screen resolution, you may not see much of the action as this is a small-resolution game. Instead, choose Run > Application or press F8 to see the running game (Figure 10.32).

CHAPTER REVIEW

We have a functional game at this time, but it lacks several things. In fact, if you play the game, you'll quickly see that there are several things that we have left to do in order to create a more playable game, and we need to add features to make it playable on an iOS device. In the next chapter, we'll continue working on this game. We are mainly going to focus on iOS-centric changes such as movement because these devices do not have a keyboard or mouse. As such, this is a very important step in the development of the game.

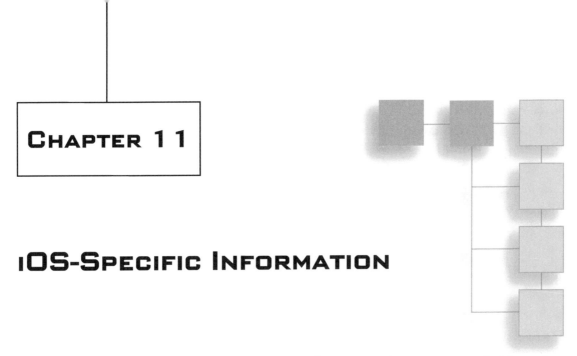

CHAPTER 11

iOS-Specific Information

In Chapter 10, we started the development of a game. There are several things that remain to make it a game playable on iOS devices. In this chapter, we'll focus on what makes an iOS application different from a PC application and mention some workarounds that you can do to keep your application working well. We'll also look at iOS-specific extensions in MMF and then create movement of the paddle for our game.

Things to Know When Creating an iOS Application

This section contains some important things to know when you create an application for the iPhone or the iPad. Please read it carefully and keep it in mind when programming your application.

Building for Various Devices

Multimedia Fusion 2 Developer allows you to build applications that can run on an iPhone, iPod Touch, or iPad. As a default, the properties of the XCode project are set to iPhone/iPad, meaning that your application will work on any of the available Apple devices.

If you want to restrict your application to iPod only, in XCode, right-click on the name of your project in the project window (topmost item) and choose "Get info." This will display the properties of the project. Scroll down a few pages until you find the line called "Targeted Device Family." Select iPod in the combo box.

If you want your application to only work on an iPad, select iPad in the combo box.

Memory Considerations

iOS devices are portable devices. As such, the amount of useable memory (RAM, not to be confused with the amount of Flash memory where the files are stored) is limited. On a 2nd-Gen device (iOS devices are at generation 4 at the time of writing), like the original iPhone and the iPod 2nd-Gen, the size of RAM is 128 Mbytes. On 3rd-Gen devices (iPhone 3 and iPod Touch 2nd-Gen) and over, the amount of RAM is 256 Mbytes. This might seem a lot, but if you know that iOS 4 consumes at least 80 Mbytes to function, you quickly realize that the amount of working memory on a 2nd-Gen device can be evaluated to around 40 Mbytes. The code of an iOS application must be copied into RAM before being launched by iOS, which takes 2 Mbytes out of your previous RAM.

The conclusion is that, if you want your application to work on a 2nd-Gen device, you have to be very careful about the size of your graphics and sounds. The next chapter of this book will provide tips to reduce the memory imprint of your graphics.

If your game cannot run on such a device, then you should prevent it from being distributed in the app store for a 2nd-Gen device. If you do so, you also save some memory by setting the build architecture of the application in the project properties to Arm7 only, avoiding the duplication of the compiled code.

Find the Memory Your App Takes

The amount of memory used by an application is shown in the debugger window (top-left of the screen) when you launch your application in Multimedia Fusion 2 Developer. The memory displayed is evaluated for a PC application, and does not reflect the amount of RAM really taken by your application under iOS.

To find out exactly how much memory your application needs on the device, in XCode, launch your application by choosing the menu option "Run/Run with performance tools/Allocations." XCode will automatically open a window that keeps track in real time of all the memory allocations of your application. You will find the total amount of RAM used in the first line of the grid.

Be sure to check every frame of your application, as the amount of memory used depends on the amount of graphics and sounds used in each frame. Also check that the number of allocations (not the temporary allocations that keep growing normally) does not increase as your game runs (and might indicate undestroyed objects). An undestroyed object is something in your game that is active, such as an enemy player. Placing them off the screen does not destroy them, so please keep this in mind as you are creating your games. When you are finished with an object, destroy it to conserve memory.

Graphics Limitations for iOS Devices

There are some limitations that you need to keep in mind when dealing with graphics for iOS devices. As always, space is a premium for mobile devices, so this information will help you to keep your applications and games running with the least amount of resources.

Alpha-Channels

Alpha-channels help create the look of transparency and can make your graphics look awesome by providing a visually pleasing effect, but they will slow down your game if you overuse them, just as they do in the PC runtime (just more).

An image with an alpha-channel takes 33% more memory and space than an image without and it takes more power and time to render them.

An easy way to work around the limitation is to check to see if the background underneath it ever changes. If not, you could probably create your image so that it combines the background and the image. That way, it simulates an alpha-channel without really requiring it.

Huge Pictures

Many are often tempted to import really large pictures into the game where it will only show very little of that picture at one time. Break it up into smaller parts so that fewer of them are shown at one time. Remember that any image you include in your game has to fit inside its own texture. In a sample game there was a 960 × 480–sized background image on a frame. This picture alone had to fit into a 1024 × 512 texture, taking up a huge amount of memory. What was even worse was that it had an alpha-channel even though no pixel in it was transparent.

Second, the same frame had two different huge animations sized 957 × 158 (each of them contained 17 frames). This already takes up 2*17 * 1024*256 * 3 = 26738688 bytes = 25.5 MB of RAM, which is way above what the iOS likes. That was even without the rest of the graphics and the huge background image we talked about before.

Most graphics don't need 100% crispness and quality. It will only take ¼th of the previous memory usage if you cut your image size in half and then at runtime scale it to 2.0. It will also run much faster as it utilizes the graphics card RAM cache more efficiently.

Image Creation Tips

Crop your images, and remove any useless empty space around them. Some developers tend to use a single frame size for an entire animation with huge transparent parts in some images. It's probably better at design time, but at runtime it results in a loss of time and space.

Try to make your graphics of a size close to something of a power-of-two. It will waste less precious memory. A power of two size is one of the following: 8,16,32,64,128,256,512,1024. Images less than 8 × 8 pixels will be stored in an 8 × 8 texture as they cannot be smaller than that. You can easily use different sizes for your width and height; they don't have to be equal.

Be sure to set the Image Compression property to Color Reduction, either globally for all objects in the App iOS properties or per object, as often as you can. You can do this in MMF or in your graphics application (like GIMP) when you create them.

In many cases it will make it consume half the memory it did before. Take for example the big background image before when it wasted 2 MB of texture memory. With color compression and no alpha-channel it will only take 1 MB. And if it was cropped to only fill out the resolution of the iPhone device, it would only take 30 KB.

The animations mentioned before that took 25 MB of RAM can, with color compression and half the resolution, only take: 2*17 * 512*128 * 2 = 4456448 bytes = 4.25 MB! That is a huge difference.

Speed Considerations

Overuse of "text" counters/score and strings, though it may not be as big of a performance issue, can hurt your game's performance a little bit if you use too many objects that draw text. If the text doesn't change it should not be a performance problem, but if you update your string/score/counters often (as counters/scores often do) you will experience a performance problem.

Here are some steps you can use for a workaround:

- Only use text whenever you know it will not change often (like every frame).

- Use bitmap counters/scores instead of text counters/scores. There you can also much better control the visual style of your objects and there is nearly no performance penalty.

Too Many Transitions

Each object that needs to have a transition effect on it will consume more memory than usual and will use some special buffers on the device that aren't unlimited. Once you reach a certain limit, you will begin getting errors. Also, if you have many transitions going on at one time, it will slow down performance.

Here are some steps you can use for a workaround:

- Instead of using transitions, try using animations or other effects to give the same effect.

- Instead of using the Fade transition, manually setting the semi-transparency of your objects will be much faster and will not consume any more memory. You can set the transparency of objects in their editors inside MMF. For example, you can double-click an active object to open its editor and set the transparency.

Unnecessary Ink Effects

Be careful to not use ink effects unnecessarily. Including a big background covering the screen and setting it to either Transparent or Add so that it will be added to some gradient behind it, will only make your game slower and consume more power. Instead, make your graphics as they should look at runtime, and then use them like that.

Ink effects are only meant for places where you cannot modify the original image to look like it should at edit time. For example, if you want a grayscale background from a picture, you make it grayscale before you import it into MMF2. You simply don't put the monochrome ink effect on it and forget about it.

Differences Between iOS and PC Applications

Multimedia Fusion 2 Developer offers you two ways of playing sounds. The first one, called "AudioPlayer," is suitable for long sounds, like background music. Its main advantage is that it does not store the entire sound in memory prior to playing, thus taking less space. Its disadvantage is that it takes some processing power when the sound is started, slowing down the application. This time lag makes it a bad choice for playing in-game sounds.

The second one, called "OpenAL," is suitable for short sounds. It does need the sound to be stored in memory prior to playing, but it does not take any processing power when the sound is started. OpenAL is a good choice for short sounds in the middle of the game.

When you use a "Play sample" action in iOS mode, you have a new check box at your disposal, named "Play with AudioPlayer." This check box has three states:

- **Unchecked.** The sound will be played using OpenAL.

- **Checked.** The sound will be played using AudioPlayer.

- **Undetermined.** Multimedia Fusion 2 Developer looks at the duration of the sound.

If it is less than 15 seconds, then it is played with OpenAL; if it is more than 15 seconds, it is played with AudioLayer. This is the automatic mode. The default setting is automatic mode. Basically, you should check the box only for background music, or leave it undetermined. Please note that the Set Sample Position action works with AudioPlayer, but not with OpenAL (except for position 0), and that the Set Sample Frequency action works only with OpenAL.

iOS supports MP3 sounds. The iPhone exporter for Multimedia Fusion 2 Developer adds an MP3 filter, to allow you to insert MP3 sounds into your applications. Be careful though, the iPhone/iPad/iPod have a single MP3 hardware decoder, so you should use MP3 sounds only for background music and do not play several MP3 sounds at the same time. You can also use the new MP3 filter to play MP3 sounds in your Windows applications, however, this filter just calls the decoding API of Windows, so it depends on codecs that are installed on the user's machine (Windows is usually provided with an MP3 codec though). Note: if you redistribute an application that contains MP3 sounds, you may need to get an MP3 license (at the date this documentation was written, a license was not required for any entity with an MP3-related gross revenue less than $100,000, but the terms of this license may change; check them from time to time on mp3licensing.com).

Edit Object

The iOS runtime supports the Edit object, but you must be aware that only a few properties of the object are supported under iOS:

- Multiple-lines

- Border, only for single-line objects

- Editable, only for single-line objects

- Vertical scroll bar, only for multiple-line objects

- Text and background Color_Object font

The object also uses the standard iOS keyboards, and is automatically positioned in the center of the screen above the keyboard when editing. If you want a finer control on the objects, just use the iOS Single Line Edit object or the iOS Multiple Lines Edit object.

Running the Application on Various Devices

Multimedia Fusion 2 Developer does its best to allow your application to run on various screen sizes from iPhone to iPad.

If the window size of the application is smaller than the device screen size, the application is zoomed and centered in the display. You do not need to change anything, and the process is completely transparent to you (screen and touch coordinates are zoomed). For example, it is perfectly possible to run a 320 × 480 application on an iPad.

If the window size of the application is bigger than the device screen size, the application is reduced and centered on the device screen. Here, too, the process is completely transparent to you. It is perfectly possible to run an iPad application (768 × 1024) on a 3rd-Gen iPhone (320 × 480).

If the application is the same size as the device screen, the application is displayed without zoom. The auto-zooming feature of Multimedia Fusion 2 Developer allows you to create applications in the best possible resolution without having to bother about which device it will run on. As an example, if you are creating for an iPhone, you can choose a window size of 640 × 960—it will be higher on a 4th-Gen iPhone and will also work fine on a 3rd- and 2nd-Gen iPhone.

Fonts

PC fonts are replaced by their iOS equivalent when running on the device. Some things to keep in mind:

- Some of the fonts do not contain Italic or Bold, or both at the same time.
- The Helvetica font is mapped to the system font on iOS (which is a Helvetica font by the way). So if you prefer to use the system font, choose Helvetica on the PC. The system font can be bold or italic but not at the same time.
- If a font does not exist on iOS, it's replaced by the system font.

String Objects

The fonts on iOS do not have exactly the same size as their PC equivalent. You might have to enlarge the string objects so that the text is displayed properly.

Old Device Limitations with the HWA Exporter

3G and 2G iPhones and iPods (3GS and up aren't affected) have some limitations when it comes to the HWA (Hardware Accelerated) blending modes. HWA simply means that the device's hardware helps with the rendering of graphics.

iOS-Specific Properties

When you choose one of the iOS build types in the Properties panel's Settings tab, new properties appear. Here is a list of the new properties.

Application Properties

These properties are located in an iOS Options tab on the far right of the Properties panel like other properties in MMF.

Bundle Identifier   This property contains the bundle identifier of your application. It should be in the form of "com.yourcompany.ApplicationName" if you follow Apple's recommendation. When you create your provisioning profile (more on this in a later chapter when we actually build an application), we strongly suggest that you enter a name like "com.yourcompany.*"; notice the * at the end, so that the provisioning profile works for more than one application.

The bundle identifier is needed to test your application on the device connected to your Mac, and furthermore to publish your application on the App Store. Please read Apple's documentation.

Image Compression   The graphic memory on iOS devices is relatively limited. The image compression option allows you to reduce the size of the graphics of your application in memory. Two options are available: None and Color Reduction. If you select Color Reduction, then the images are automatically converted to 65536 colors (opaque images), 32768 colors (unique transparent color), or 4096 colors (alpha-channel with multiple transparency levels). This option will divide the size of your images by 2. This can reduce the quality of the images though, but you can choose to ignore this option for specific objects.

Multitask   iOS 4 is a multitasking environment. If, when you use an application, you press the HOME button on the device, the application is put into sleep mode and taken to the background. You can revive it by clicking on it in the application list. Perhaps you don't want your application to multitask; in this case, untick this property, and your application will be discarded when the user presses HOME. I would not recommend this as Apple prefers multitasking apps.

Application Icon   This property contains the icon of your application. It is a 114 × 144 image that will be used to display your application on the device. Click Edit to modify it. Please note that the Reflection effect will be automatically added by the device; you do not need (and must not or your application will be rejected by Apple) to add such an effect; your icon must be "flat."

Launch Image   This property contains the image to be displayed on the device while the application is loading. It should be a title picture, or the representation of the first frame of your application. It should encourage the user to be patient and wait. This is a 640 × 480 picture.

iTunes Artwork   This property contains the image to be used in iTunes. It is a 512 × 512 image and should be the same as the application icon (otherwise Apple will reject your application). Here too, you should not add any Reflection effect.

Enable iAd   Enable iAd allows the use of iAd banners in your application. This section may only be useful for those with Multimedia Fusion Developer edition.

Display Ad on the Bottom of the Screen   Positions the ad in the bottom of the screen instead of the top. You might be surprised to see that the size of the icon, launch, and artwork images is double the normal size of an iPhone 3rd-Gen. With iPhone's 4th-Gen running in 640 × 480, a higher resolution of the system images is needed. Multimedia Fusion 2 Developer automatically creates two versions of the images when it saves the project, one in 320 × 480 and one in 640 × 480 so that it runs on any device.

Frame Properties   Frame properties specific to iOS show up under the iOS Options tab in the far right of the Properties panel when a frame is selected in the Frame Editor.

Touch Mode   Choose between Single Touch and Multi Touch. If Single Touch is selected, only one finger (the first one on the screen) will be detected. If you use the Multi Touch object, multiple touches will be detected. Please note that the latter option needs more battery power, so you should only use it when necessary.

The first touches (or single touches) are automatically mapped to the mouse pointer coordinate in Multimedia Fusion 2 Developer, so you can create applications using the mouse with no problem.

Screen Locking   If your game does not induce the user to touch the screen (use of accelerometers, or static frames), the device might go automatically, after a period of time, into energy-saving mode, reducing the lighting of the screen and then shutting off.

You can prevent this from happening by checking the screen locking property. If checked, the device will remain ON at full power for the duration of the frame. Please use this property with caution, as it might drain the user's battery!

Joystick/Device   Multimedia Fusion 2 Developer allows you to emulate a joystick in the iOS application. With this, you can use Multimedia Fusion 2 Developer default movements, controlled by a joystick on the device. This combo box offers you the choice of joysticks:

- **None.** No joystick is displayed. Only use this property when your frame does not contain any joystick-controlled movement.

- **Touch joystick.** The joystick is emulated on the bottom of the screen of the device. Using your fingers, you can control the movements. The joystick consists of a paddle button and two fire buttons that can be repositioned or made invisible.

- **Accelerometers.** The movements are controlled by the position of the device. Two fire buttons are available on the screen.

- **Controlled by an extension.** Choose this property to manually start or stop the joystick using the Joystick Control object. Please note that this object will not work if this property is not set to this value.

- **Fire 1 button.** Check this box if you want the Fire 1 button to be displayed.

- **Fire 2 button.** Check this box if you want the Fire 2 button to be displayed.

- **Left handed.** Check this box to have the paddle on the right and the fire buttons on the left of the screen.

Display Ad   Displays (if possible) the iAd banner. If unchecked, no banner is displayed. The images used by the joystick are simple, semi-transparent pictures that can be found in the Resources folder of the XCode project. Feel free to modify them to your liking.

Object Properties   Object properties specific to iOS show up under the iOS Options tab in the far right of the Properties panel whenever an object is selected in a frame. The properties available depend on the version of MMF that you have.

Image Compression   Image compression allows you to force the compression mode of the object's images with the following three options:

- **Default.** The Image Compression mode of the application will be used. Refer to the properties of the application above for more info.

- **None.** The images of the object won't be compressed even if the Image Compression property of the application is set to Color Reduction.

- **Color Reduction.** The images of the object will be compressed even if the Image Compression property of the application is set to None.

iOS Movement Example

Now that you have an overview of some of the differences in iOS and regular PC development using MMF, we will look at how to update our project to include the capabilities of movement using iOS-specific objects.

There are a couple of ways to create the movement for the paddle in our project. First, we can use the Joystick Control object. It's an excellent component that displays a virtual joystick anywhere you want on an iOS device. The other option is to use the Accelerometer, which means that you can control the paddle by movement of the iOS device in whatever way you decide. For this example, we'll build it with the Joystick Control.

To get started, open the project from Chapter 10 in MMF. Next, choose Insert > New Object in the frame editor. You should see a window like Figure 11.1.

Move down the list of objects (you can view all objects in alphabetical order by clicking All Objects on the left so that it is easier to locate a specific object) to locate the Joystick Control object. Double-click it and place it on your frame as shown in Figure 11.2.

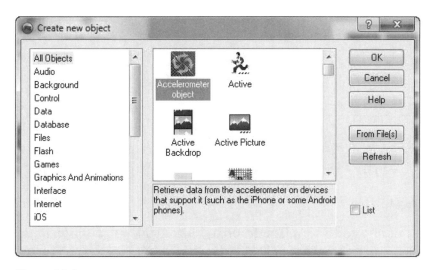

Figure 11.1
Create New Object window.

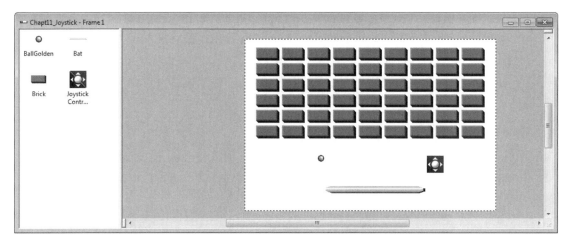

Figure 11.2
The Joystick Control.

Figure 11.3
The Storybook condition is selected.

Next, open the Event Editor and add a New Condition by clicking New Condition in the list of events. Double-click the Storybook condition, which looks like a chess piece and board (Figure 11.3). When you double-click the storybook condition, you will see a menu that allows you to choose Start of Frame. Click the Start of Frame to create the event.

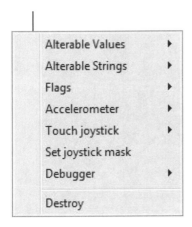

Figure 11.4
The menu appears when you right-click.

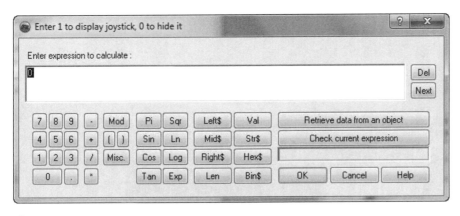

Figure 11.5
The first step in creating the joystick display.

Now that we have an event, the next step is to right-click on the square box that is beneath the Joystick Object and to the right of the Start of Frame condition you just added. When you right-click, you should see something like Figure 11.4.

Choose Touch Joystick > Start/stop touch joystick. You will see a window like Figure 11.5. Enter a value of 1 to display the joystick and click OK. The next window looks like Figure 11.6. The Virtual Joystick can display two buttons. We don't have a need for it in this game, but if you were building a game that needed them, they are built-in. You can enter a 0, and then click OK. Another window that is identical to Figure 11.6 is displayed, but this window is used for setting options for the second button. You can enter a 0 and then click OK. The last step is

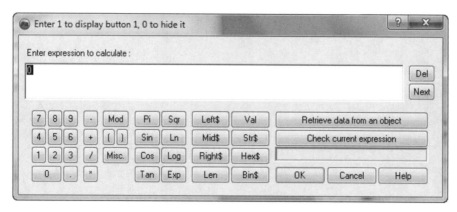

Figure 11.6
The second of four steps.

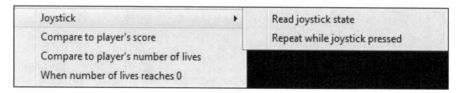

Figure 11.7
Choose Controlled by an extension.

Figure 11.8
Joystick conditions.

another window; this time it is for orientation of the joystick as either right-handed or left-handed. You can enter a 0 for right-handed and click OK.

The next step is to make a quick change in the Frame Properties window. Click Frame 1 in the Workspace Toolbar to select that frame. Its properties will appear in the Properties panel to the right. Go to the iOS Options tab in the Properties panel. Next to Device, use the drop-down selection to choose Controlled by an extension, as seen in Figure 11.7.

With those settings complete, you need to go back to the Events Editor. Click the New Condition button and then double-click the icon that looks like a joystick. You will see a menu that looks like Figure 11.8.

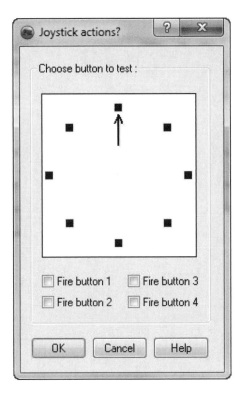

Figure 11.9
The Joystick Actions window.

From the menu, choose Joystick > Read joystick state. You will see a window like Figure 11.9 that represents the direction of the joystick. Click the square to the left so that it looks like Figure 11.10. Click the OK button. You will now see a Moved Left entry as an event.

Right-click the square that is below the Bat object and to the right of the newly created Moved Left action. From the menu that appears, choose Position > Set X Coordinate, which will display something like Figure 11.11.

Click the "Retrieve data from an object" button and from the list of objects that appear, you can double-click the Bat object, which will display a menu. From this menu, choose Position > X Coordinate. You will now see the Set X Coordinate window has a new expression that says X ("bat"). (See Figure 11.12.) To move the bat left, we want to take the current position of the bat and then subtract a value, which in our case is 6. You can play around with the values when you test them out to see if the movement needs to be slower or faster and then change the value to a larger or shorter number. When you add the −6 after the expression, click the OK button.

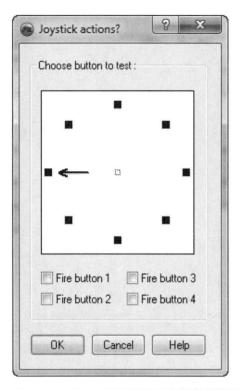

Figure 11.10
The window with left selected.

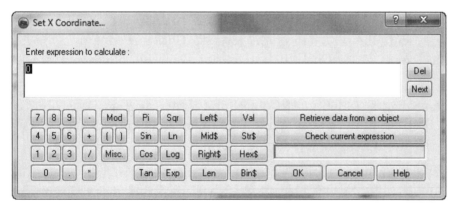

Figure 11.11
Set X Coordinate window.

Now, we need to repeat this for the right direction. You can either go through all of the steps individually, or you can create a new Joystick move right event, and then drag and drop the check box that represents the left movement action into the right movement line. If you do this, double-click the newly copied action and then change

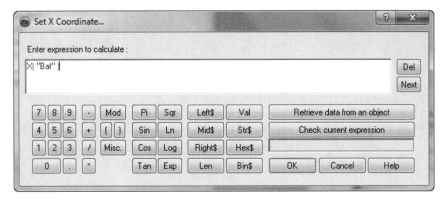

Figure 11.12
The expression has changed.

it from a −6 to a +6 so that if you push the joystick to the right, it will move right and not left.

CHAPTER REVIEW

In this chapter, you learned some of the differences between developing for the iOS and regular games in MMF. You also continued the project we started in Chapter 10 to create a playable game for an iOS device. In the next chapter, you will learn how to add this project to an iOS device and/or emulator for testing.

CHAPTER 12

DEPLOYING TO AN iOS DEVICE OR EMULATOR

In order to go on to the next step, you need to download the iPhone SDK from http://developer.apple.com. At the time of this writing, the current SDK is version 4.2. If you download a different version, your screens may look slightly different than those shown in this chapter. While the screens in future versions of the SDK may be slightly different, the principles of the instructions should be helpful.

Once you download the SDK, double-click the DMG file and then select Xcode from the window that appears.

Click Continue through screens that look like Figure 12.1 through 12.8

TESTING AND DEPLOYING TO A REAL DEVICE

Now that you have Xcode installed, the next step, before you can copy your MMF program to a real device, is to complete the App Store registration with Apple. Until you do this, you will not be able to complete the provisioning process.

Building Your iOS Application

Let's move back to the PC to see how to move your project over to Xcode on the Mac. First, create your application or game on your PC (or open the one we just finished in Chapter 11), making sure that "iOS Xcode project" is selected in the Build types properties of the application. Test the application on the PC.

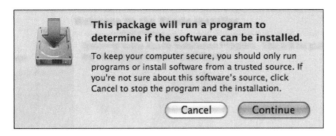

Figure 12.1
Installing the iOS SDK.

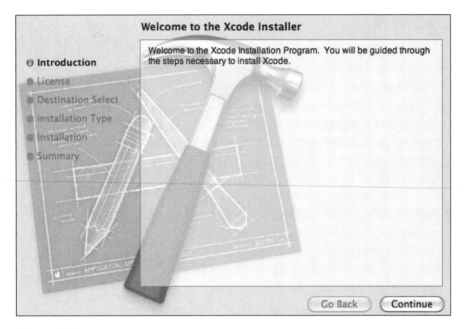

Figure 12.2
Installing the iOS SDK.

Choose File > Build > Application and enter the name of your zipped Xcode project (should be the same name as the application plus the ZIP extension).

Developer saves a ZIP file containing a complete Xcode project ready to compile.

Transferring the ZIP File on Your Mac

It was mentioned early in the book how you could use online services such as Dropbox, a network, a memory stick, or a CD/DVD to transfer files between a Mac and PC. Using the method that you prefer, copy the ZIP file from the Mac to the PC and

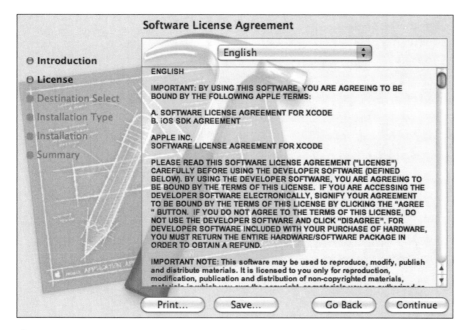

Figure 12.3
Installing the iOS SDK.

Figure 12.4
Installing the iOS SDK.

then unzip the ZIP file on your Mac by simply double-clicking on it. You now have a complete Xcode project folder.

Starting Xcode Using Finder or Spotlight

Open the "XXX.xcodeproj" file in Xcode, where XXX is the name of your application. You can do this by double-clicking the file. For the first build, select Simulator in the top-left drop-down menu (Figure 12.9), which displays a variety of options for deployment,

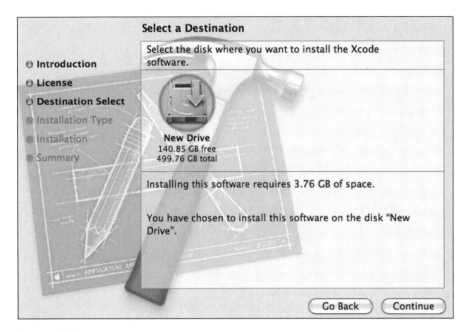

Figure 12.5
Installing the iOS SDK.

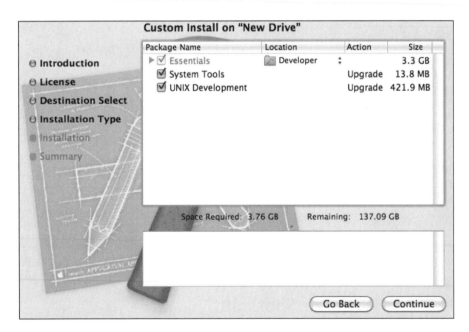

Figure 12.6
Installing the iOS SDK.

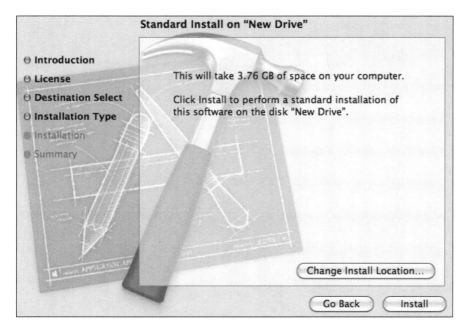

Figure 12.7
Installing the iOS SDK.

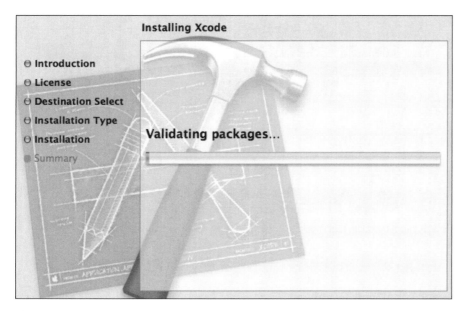

Figure 12.8
Installing the iOS SDK.

Figure 12.9
Select Simulator from the drop-down.

Figure 12.10
Application running in emulator.

including an iOS device that will be covered later. If "Base SDK missing" is displayed in the combo box, open the project settings and change the Base SDK option.

Click on "Build and run." After a little time, the emulator should start and display your application. It will look like Figure 12.10.

Now that you have a working Xcode project on your Mac, there is no need to transfer the entire project each time want to test your application. There is a much easier method provided by Multimedia Fusion 2 Developer.

- In the Application properties on the PC, open "Build type" and select iOS application (cci).

- Build your application as usual, but as a file name enter "Application.cci." This will save a file called "Application.cci."

- Transfer "Application.cci" to your Mac.

- On the Mac, copy this file to the root of your Xcode folder.

- Then in Xcode, recompile the project. The new application is used.

When the development is over, and you are publishing your final application, select Application properties on the PC, then "Build type," and select "iOS final Xcode project." Build your application, entering the name of an Xcode zipped folder and then follow these steps:

- Transfer the ZIP file to your Mac.

- Double-click on the ZIP to unzip it.

- Open the file "XXX.xcodeproj" in Xcode, where XXX is the name of your application.

- Build and run the application.

To publish your application, you will need to follow Apple's exact procedures, which can be found in the developer documentation. Before we move on, you might be wondering what the difference is between the "iOS Xcode project" and the "iOS final Xcode project"?

The difference resides in the extensions. The development project contains all the available extensions, and therefore works if you add a new extension to your application, allowing you to copy the cci file directly to the folder of the Xcode project. The final project only contains the necessary extensions, making the file size smaller. The counterpart is that it will crash if you add a new extension.

Using a Device

Now that it works in the simulator, let's get it working on our device. First, connect your iOS device to your Mac. In Xcode, change the drop-down so that instead of attempting to run the program in the simulator, Xcode will run the program on an actual device. When you attempt to run the program, you'll get a failure notice stating that the device doesn't have a provisioning profile. If you select Install and Run from the error dialog, you'll encounter another failure about the provisioning profile not being found.

Click the Add to Portal button. It will ask for your Apple account password and then it will offer to request a certificate for you. You can refresh the Provisioning Profiles section until a valid "Team Provisioning Profile: *" pops up there. The icon should turn green next to the device.

Using Add to Portal does a number of things for you automatically:

■ It creates a developer certificate for you, which includes a public/private keypair that is added to your OS X keychain. iOS apps need to be signed to run on the device and your key will be used to sign your app for testing purposes.

■ The next thing it does is upload a request to sign the certificate to the Apple iOS Provisioning Portal. Your certificate needs to be signed by Apple, otherwise the app will not run on the device.

■ The Unique Device ID (UDID) of your device is added to the iOS Provisioning Portal.

■ Creates an App ID in the iOS Provisioning Portal.

■ Creates a Provisioning Profile in the iOS Provisioning Portal. This is the permission to run apps (having a matching App ID) signed with your key on only the devices with the specified UDIDs.

■ Downloads the provisioning profile from the iOS Provisioning Portal and installs it to Xcode and on your phone.

Once complete, in Xcode, you can pick the hardware device in the Scheme selector (Figure 12.11) and run the app on the hardware device.

Figure 12.11
The Scheme selector in Xcode.

You should be able to run the project on your device now. Every now and then, when I go through the process of deploying the provisioning certificate to the device, it doesn't work. When this happens, I have to disconnect and then reconnect my iDevice once or twice before it will work. This doesn't happen often, but just be aware that it could happen.

CHAPTER REVIEW

In this chapter we installed the iOS SDK, and learned how to transfer applications from Multimedia Fusion 2 to Xcode so that they can be tested on devices or in the simulator. In the next chapter, we'll get back to creating games in MMF by working on an arcade-style space game.

CHAPTER 13

CREATING AN iOS SPACE GAME

You have covered a large amount of ground leading up to this chapter. You have learned how to set up a small studio for your projects, how to design a project including a basic design document, create game graphics, create music, and assemble the entire package of components in MMF. In this chapter, we'll create a game project for iOS devices.

STARTING THE PROJECT

To get started, we have already created a nice space backdrop, so as far as graphics go, there really isn't much to do. We can use some of the built-in spaceship graphics in MMF to quickly assemble our game.

For background music, MMF's built-in sound effects should work well for things like explosions and lasers.

In Appendix E, we have a list of great locations on the web that you can find free resources for graphics, music, and sound effects.

MMF

The creation of a space game begins in MMF. Open it and then create an application using the following parameter:

Build Type: iOS XCode Project

When you create the application as an XCode project, you will be presented with the Window Size dialog box that looks like Figure 13.1.

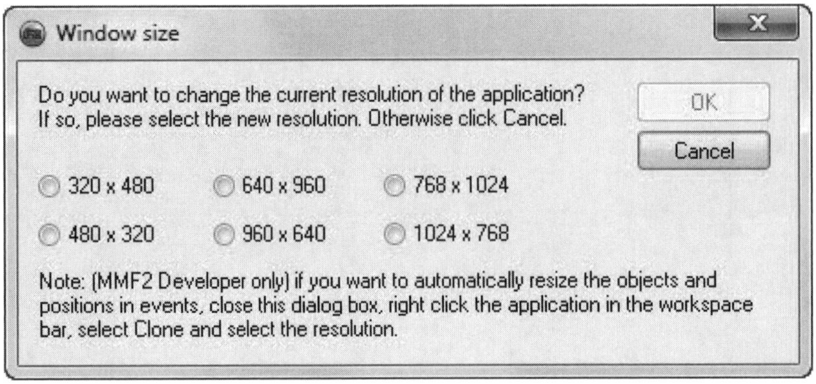

Figure 13.1
You need to choose a screen resolution.

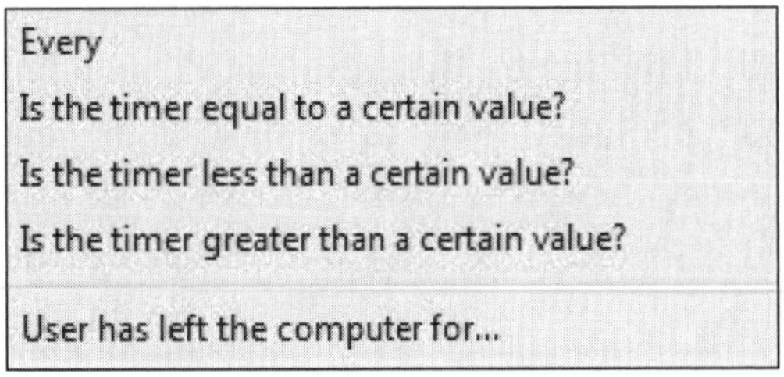

Figure 13.2
The options for the Timer.

From this dialog, select 960 × 640 as it will display correctly for new devices as well as old. You have the first frame available for editing. Click the Number 1 on the left side to open Frame 1 in the Frame Editor. You can create a nice splash screen using the Gimp or other editor, but for this example, I'm simply going to place some text on the screen for 5 seconds. You can use this as a splash screen when you create your own game.

For our example, we've chosen to add a Text String object and added "Splash Screen" as the paragraph text. Obviously this is not how you will want to leave it for a game you want to distribute. You should create a nice background using the techniques you already learned.

Open the Event Editor, which at this time is empty. Double-click New Condition, and from the window that opens, double-click the Timer, which will display another menu that looks like Figure 13.2.

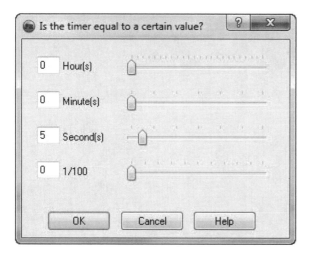

Figure 13.3
Setting the time to 5 seconds.

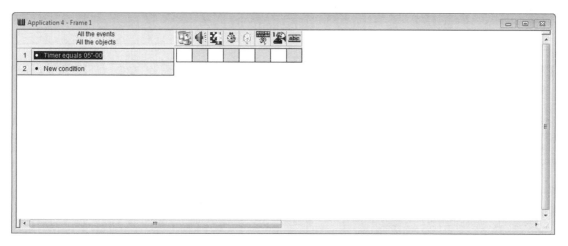

Figure 13.4
Choose Next Frame.

Choose "Is the Timer Equal to a Certain Value" and from the window that opens (see Figure 13.3 for an example), choose a time frame that you would like, such as the 5 seconds shown in the example.

Once you have an event, we need to create the action that occurs when the event is triggered. Right-click the box beneath the icon that looks like a chess board. From the menu, which can be seen in Figure 13.4, you can choose Next Frame. This will simply move on to the next frame once 5 seconds have been reached. That's all there is to the Splash Screen. You can close the Event Editor.

Figure 13.5
The Accelerometer object can be placed anywhere.

You should now be back at the Storyboard Editor in MMF. The next step is to click "Number 2" to create a second frame for our game. This is the frame that we will use to create the game. If you wanted to create a game with multiple levels, you could simply continue creating frames for each level and use the Next Frame idea from above when you reach the end of the level. For our example, we'll create only a single frame.

Click the Number 2 again to open the Frame Editor. We'll use the Accelerometer to move our ship. You can add the Accelerometer to the project by choosing Insert > New Object and locating the Accelerometer and double-clicking it. You can place the object inside or outside the frame, as it is not shown at runtime (see Figure 13.5).

Next, insert a Counter object and name its position (Figure 13.6). When using the Accelerometer, you will often need to adjust values to get the right feel for your game. Next, add a new active object, which will be our ship. You can add a better game graphic, but in the example, I simply resized the standard diamond shape object, double-clicked it, and shaved off the bottom to make a rudimentary ship (Figure 13.7). We've designed space objects earlier in the book, so this should be a relatively easy add for you. You can add an additional active object as a laser beam and rename both objects to represent what they are in the game: Ship and Laser.

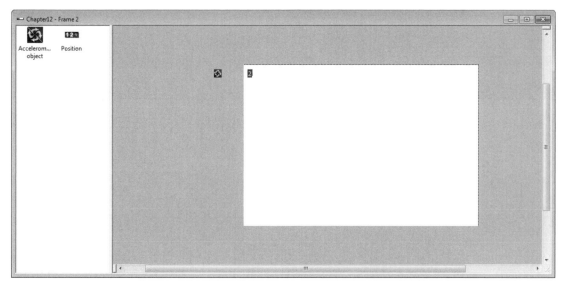

Figure 13.6
Create a new Counter object.

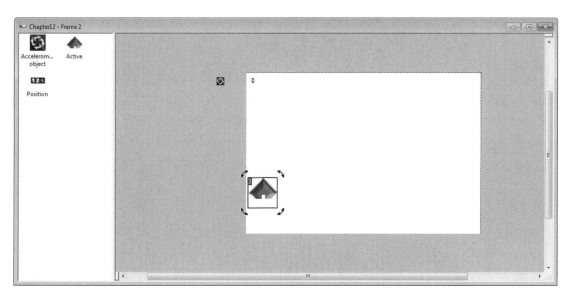

Figure 13.7
Making a simple spaceship.

Insert another active object—enemy creator. Give it a movement path by creating a new line and then drawing it so it looks like Figure 13.8.

Add another active object for the enemy ship off the screen (Figure 13.9).

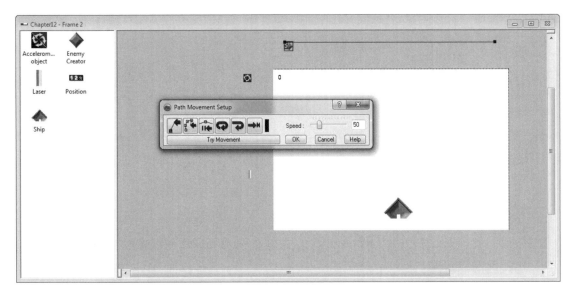

Figure 13.8
Draw similarly to this.

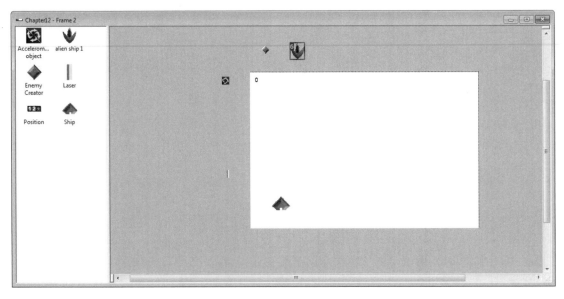

Figure 13.9
Add off screen.

Add a new system box to act as a button to fire a laser (Figure 13.10 options, Figure 13.11 position).

Now we need to create events. First, create a new event every 0.10 seconds. You can do this by double-clicking New Condition, which will display the New Conditions

Figure 13.10
Setting properties for the Fire button.

dialog. From this box, right-click the icon that looks like a Clock icon and choose Every from the list. You can now enter .10 into the 1/100 box. Right-click the box beneath Counter and to the right of the event and choose Set Counter (Figure 13.12). Click the Retrieve data from an object button to get to the screen seen in Figure 13.13. Choose Direct values > X acceleration (Figure 13.14). Set Counter now has the value XDirect("Acceleromter Object") as shown in Figure 13.15. Click OK.

Our next step is to test the value of the counter that we are using for movement. When using the Accelerometer for movement, it is a bit of trial and error to get the right "feel" for an individual game. We are going to test the value of the counter, and if it is less than −.04, we'll move our ship left and if it is greater than .04, we'll move to the right. The −.04 and .04 are values that I have tried on various devices and seem to be a good starting point. You can adjust as necessary, or create an

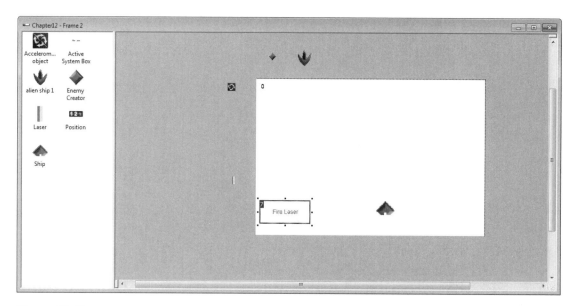

Figure 13.11
Positioned in the scene.

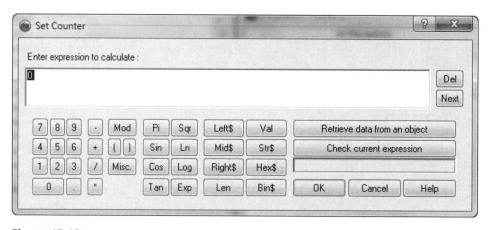

Figure 13.12
Setting the counter up.

option to allow the user to change the "feel" by creating a variable that would store their favorite value. Double-click New Condition. Double-click the Position counter and then choose Compare the Counter to a Value. Enter value of −.04 and Less Than from the drop-down (Figure 13.16). Click OK. Now, do the same thing for another event, but this time choose Greater Than from the drop-down and a value of .04 (no negative).

Figure 13.13
New expression window.

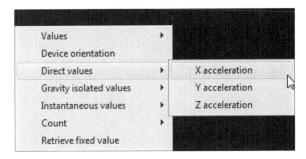

Figure 13.14
Setting the X acceleration.

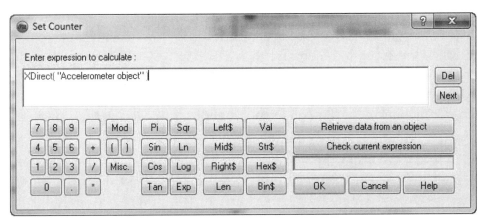

Figure 13.15
The expression is completed.

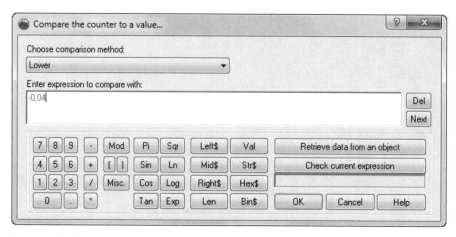

Figure 13.16
Comparing to a value.

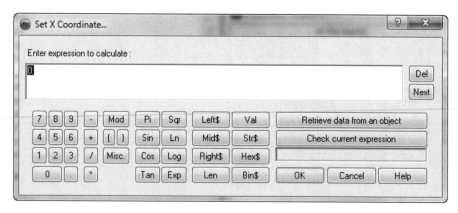

Figure 13.17
Setting X coordinate.

You now have 2 events, but we need to set the corresponding actions. For event 2 (less than −.04), right-click the box beneath the spaceship and then select Set X coordinate. A window that looks like Figure 13.17 is displayed. Click the Retrieve data from an object button. Double-click the spaceship icon and then Position > X Coordinate from the menu. The window now says X("Ship") like Figure 13.18. We need to move it to the left, so add a −4 to the end. It simply moves the ship 4 pixels to the left of where it currently sits. Do the same for moving to the right on Event 3, but this time add 4 to the X position.

Double-click New Condition. From Options, right-click the Fire button and then choose Button > Is Clicked from the pop-up menu. Right-click the square beneath the spaceship and to the right of the condition you created, and from the menu, choose Launch an Object. Choose Laser (Figure 13.19). Choose a speed of 40 (Figure 13.20). Next, you need to change the direction by clicking "Launch in

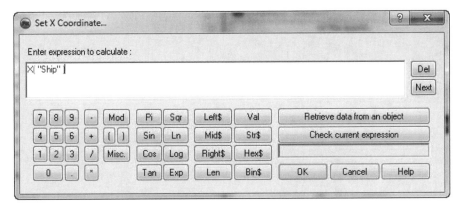

Figure 13.18
Using X value of ship.

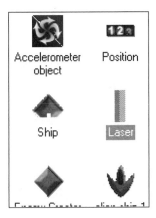

Figure 13.19
Choosing the Laser object.

Figure 13.20
Setting speed of 40.

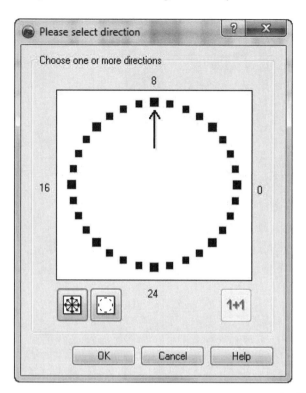

Figure 13.21
Launch in direction.

selected direction" (Figure 13.21). Point your arrow up at 8 to select the "up" direction and then click OK. Click OK again.

It's a good time to look at two things that we haven't spent time with up to this point: action points and hot spots. A *hot spot* is the point in an image that corresponds to the actual X and Y coordinates of the object. You can set the position of the hot spot in the image with the Picture Editor by double-clicking the object in the Frame Editor. If you are editing an image list, for example a direction in the Animation Editor, you move the hot spot in all the images by pressing ALT while changing the position of the hot spot.

The *action point* is the location in the image where the action takes place (for example, when you launch an object, the bullet will be created at the position of the action point). You can set the position of the action point with this tool. Like the hot spot, you can move the action point in all the images by pressing ALT while changing the position of the action point.

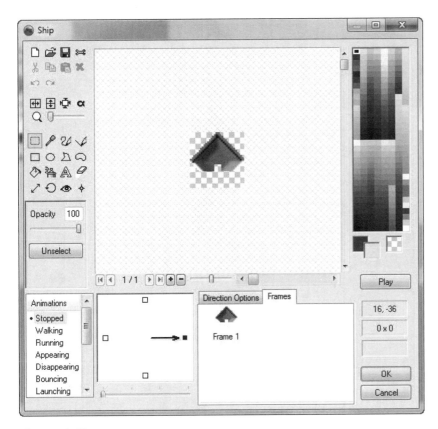

Figure 13.22
Opening the ship.

If you were to run this frame right now, the ship would fire every time that you click the Fire button. However, depending on the image you used for the ship, you need to set the action point to an appropriate location so that the laser shoots from the top of the ship. In the Frame Editor, double-click your ship (Figure 13.22). Next, click the icon at the lower right of the toolbar to display the action point (Figure 13.23). By clicking and dragging the action point, you can move the location to the middle top of the ship (Figure 13.24). Click OK to close the window and set the action point. It's basically the same steps to set the hot spot of the laser as well. You can do this by choosing View Hot Spot button, which looks like an eye, and is located directly to the left of the Hot Spot button. Once you click the View Hot Point button, the steps to move it are exactly the same as the action point. Click OK when you are finished setting both.

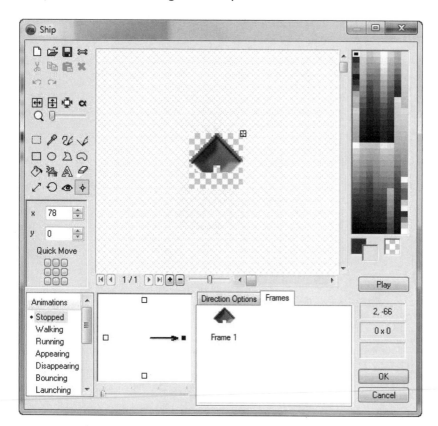

Figure 13.23
Display the action point.

Open the Event Editor and then right-click the icon that looks like a clock. From the drop-down menu, choose Every and then set the time to 3 seconds. We're going to have an enemy created every 3 seconds. We could actually change this value to create more ships as the levels proceed. In the square box beneath the Enemy Creator object we added earlier and on the same row as the event we just created, right-click and choose Launch an Object and pick the enemy ship object. For the direction, choose the directions as shown in Figure 13.25. Click OK and set the speed to 30 and click OK again.

In a real game, you might want to set the ships to move back to the top of the image and attack again if they are not struck by a laser on the way down. However, to keep this simple, we'll simply create an event to destroy them when they leave the screen.

In the Event Editor, double-click New Condition and right-click the enemy ship. Next, choose Position > Test Position from the menu. This displays the window like

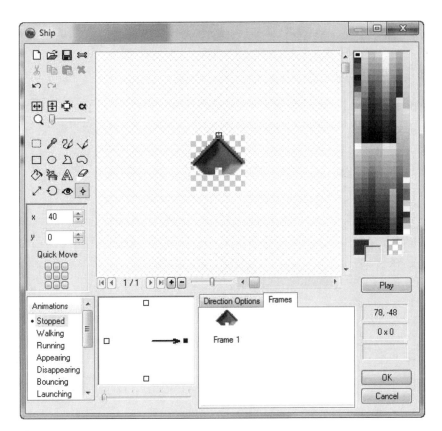

Figure 13.24
Set the correct position.

Figure 13.26. Click the left arrow, right arrow, and down arrow inside the screen area and click OK. It creates an event that reads "Enemy leaves the play area on the left, right or bottom." To the right of this event, you can find the box beneath the enemy ship. Right-click, then choose Visibility > Make Invisible. Next, right-click on the same box and choose Destroy. The reason we made the ship disappear first is so that any explosion animations would not be displayed when it is destroyed by leaving the play area. Our events now look like Figure 13.27.

We need to make an event that occurs when the laser hits the enemy ship. First, add a new Counter to the frame and call it score. Position it in the upper right like Figure 13.28. Open the Event Editor and click New Condition. From the objects, right-click on the laser and then choose Collision > Another Object. From the Test a Collision window, choose the enemy ship. Within this event, we

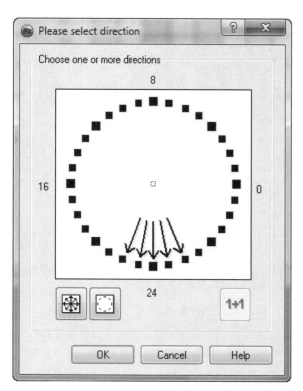

Figure 13.25
Choosing the direction.

need to add to our score and destroy the enemy. Right-click on the box beneath the new counter you created and in the row of this event. Choose Add to Counter from the menu. Enter a value of 100 and then click OK. This adds to our score. Next, right-click the square beneath the enemy ship and then choose Destroy from the options. You can also Destroy the laser in this event unless you would like it to keep moving with the ability to destroy additional ships.

Now, create the same type of collision between our ship and the enemy ship, but this time, create an event that ends the game when this occurs. You could create a number of lives for the player, or move to another level, but we'll keep it simple for this game.

You can save and run the game but you'll quickly realize that you can fire with the mouse by clicking on the Fire button, but you cannot move the ship. That's because there is not a way to emulate the Accelerometer on the PC. Instead, create a new event that uses the Joystick object and checks for left presses to move the ship. To do this, double-click the New Condition and right-click the Joystick object and choose Joystick > Repeat while joystick is pressed. This will open a new window

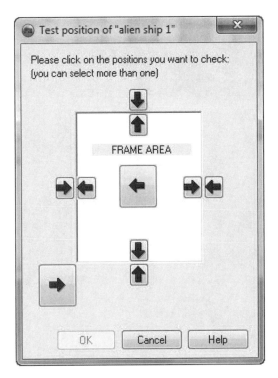

Figure 13.26
Testing the position.

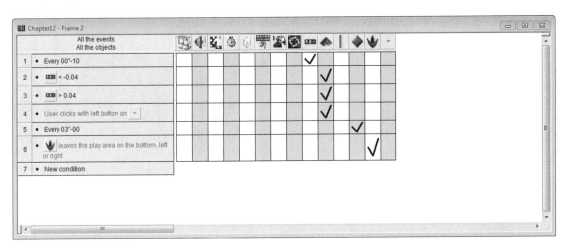

Figure 13.27
The events in the editor.

that looks like Figure 13.29. Choose the Left direction and click OK. Inside this event, right-click on the square box beneath the ship and create the same move left action that we did earlier by checking the current X position of the ship and then subtracting 4. Create a new event for the right direction and set the position by adding 4 to

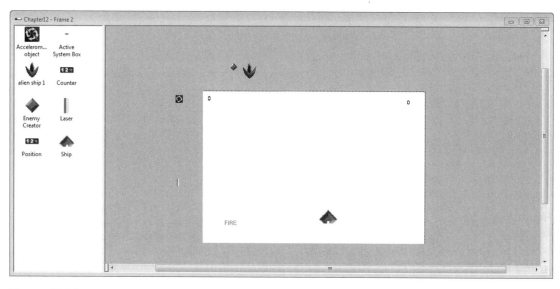

Figure 13.28
Setting the position.

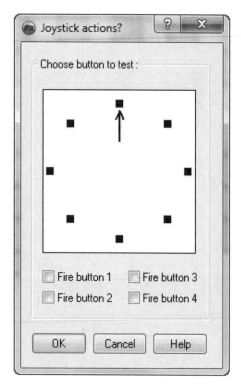

Figure 13.29
The Joystick actions.

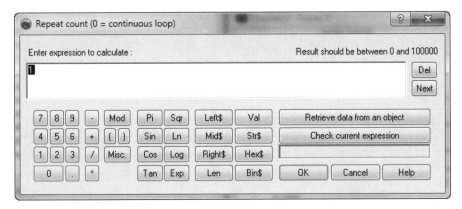

Figure 13.30
Repeat the loop.

the current X value. This movement provides a simulation of what it will be like on the iOS device. You can delete these movements when you are finished deploying to a device, but it works well for quick testing on the PC.

The final steps are to add the background and some music and sound effects. Create a new event in the Event Editor by clicking New Condition. Right-click on the object that looks like a chess board and choose Start of Frame from the menu. Add the music to this event by right-clicking the box beneath the Sound icon and choosing Play and Loop Sample from the menu. Locate the music you created earlier in the book or download a royalty-free or public domain song you'd like to use. Click the Browse button next to From a File and locate the music you'd like to use and click OK. A window that looks like Figure 13.30 is displayed. From this window, choose 0 to have the track loop over and over and then click OK. You can add sound effects in a similar manner by choosing the box next to the laser/enemy ship collision event and the ship/enemy collision. You will simply put a 1 into the number of times to play the "explosion" sound effect. You can also add a sound to the laser being fired by creating it in the event that fires the laser.

Note

Don't forget that Appendix E contains a great list of sites that you can use to get royalty-free or public domain images, sound effects, and music.

CHAPTER REVIEW

In this chapter, you used all of the information you learned so far and created a full game that can be used as a base for future projects. You could add to this game by creating new frames for levels and adding options for tracking lives and new ships.

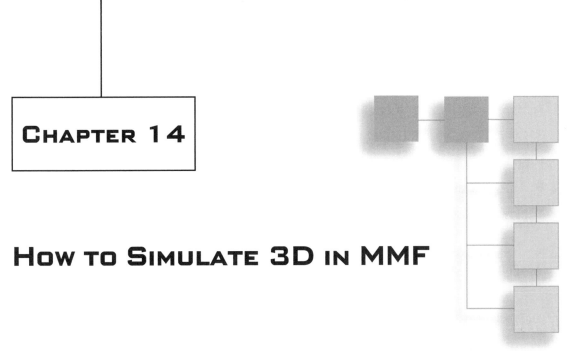

CHAPTER 14

HOW TO SIMULATE 3D IN MMF

In this chapter, we're going to take a look at some new things you can do with Multimedia Fusion, and more specifically, we are going to look at how we can simulate a 3D game environment with a tool that offers a mostly 2D set of tools.

THIRD-PARTY EXTENSIONS

There are a number of third-party extensions available to create 3D games in MMF, and because MMF allows some functionality with ActiveX controls, you can take advantage of some solutions developed for other environments such as Visual Basic. Some of the options include 3D engines like TrueVision 3D (truevision3d.com) or Summit 3D (www.summit3d.com), but I have not tried creating a full game with either of them in MMF. As mentioned, any engine that provides an ActiveX control should have the ability to be used in MMF. Other options that are also worth mentioning are the various MMF extensions that you can find on Clickteam's (www .clickteam.com) discussion forums such as the beta version of the OpenGL extension collection. You can do a search for "OpenGL collection" at clickteam.com to locate it. We'll limit our brief look at a couple of the MMF-specific extensions.

Mode 7 ex

Mode 7 ex was developed by Cellosoft (www.cellosoft.com) and is probably the best of the third-party 3D objects available for MMF. If you are a game player, you may have heard of Mode 7, a hardware graphics mode popularized by the Super Nintendo Entertainment System (SNES) for rotating and scaling images. It was mainly used for special effects and to add perspective to maps that would normally be 2D.

According to the Mode 7 ex documentation, it offers numerous improvements from the original Mode 7, including:

- Heightmap for voxel terrains
- DirectDraw compatibility
- Internal image support
- Auto-redraw handling
- New render settings: fog, interpolation, mip-mapping, wrapping
- Secondary layer
- Vitalize 3 certified!

We're not going to go through the process of creating a project with the Mode 7 object because the object is not available for iOS devices. Unfortunately, you can only use the Mode 7 ex object for projects you are creating for Windows.

SIMULATING 3D WITH THE ACTIVE PICTURE AND ACTIVE OBJECT

For iOS developers making a game in MMF, the only real option is to simulate 3D. At first glance, the use of the standard 2D Active object or Active Picture to simulate 3D may not make a great deal of sense. However, with a quick example, it's very easy to see how to take advantage of the normally 2D graphics.

Example Using Active Object

It's very easy to see how this concept will work. We can simply resize the Active Picture or Active object graphics to simulate moving toward or away from the screen. For example, to simulate an object moving away, we'll resize it to make it look smaller. Let's create a quick example. Open MMF and create a new application. It doesn't matter the size of the application as this will be a very quick example. Your empty application should look like Figure 14.1.

The next step is to open the Frame Editor, which should look like Figure 14.2.

Choose Insert > New Object to display the Create New Object window (Figure 14.3).

Double-click the Active object to add it to the frame, which should now look like Figure 14.4.

Double-click the Active object so that you can edit the image (Figure 14.5). Hold down your CTRL key and press the A key. This sequence is a shortcut for Select All.

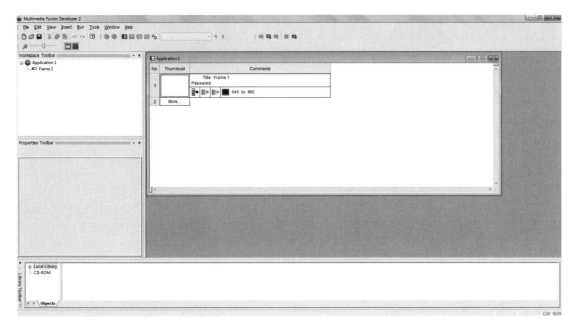

Figure 14.1
The new application in MMF.

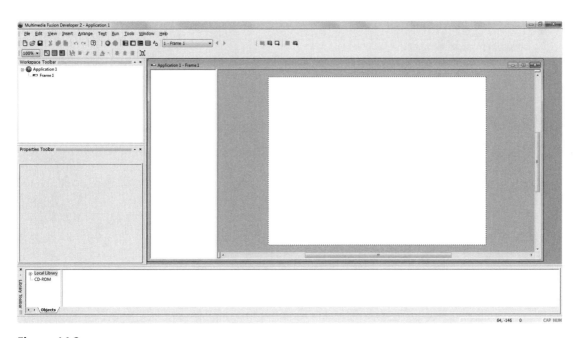

Figure 14.2
The empty frame in MMF.

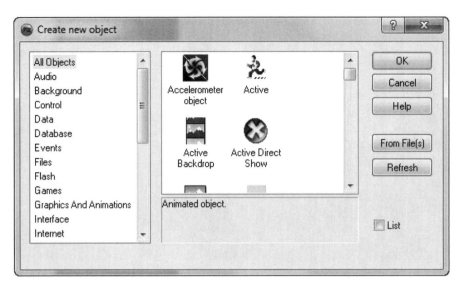

Figure 14.3
Create New Object window in MMF.

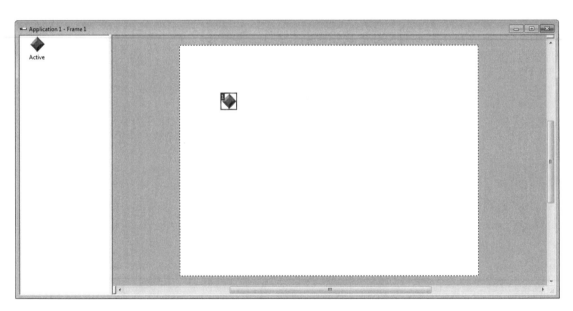

Figure 14.4
The frame has a new Active object.

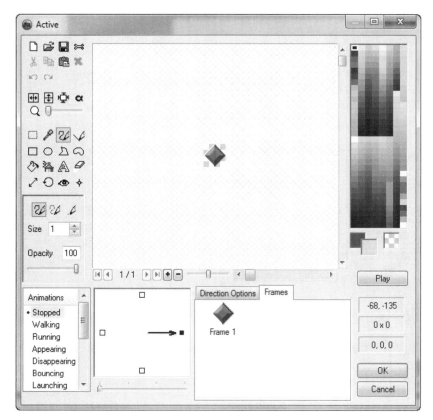

Figure 14.5
The Active object image editor.

You will see a box around the existing diamond drawing (Figure 14.6). Press the Delete key on your keyboard to erase all of the content (Figure 14.7).

The next step is to draw a circle for the image by choosing the Ellipse tool (Figure 14.8). Choose one of the shades of red in the color chooser on the right by clicking it (Figure 14.9). On the left side of the editor, choose the shaded option like Figure 14.10. Position your mouse at the upper left of the canvas and click and drag to draw a circle like Figure 14.11. It doesn't need to be perfect as any shape will actually work fine.

Click the OK button and you should see the circle represented in the Frame Editor look something like Figure 14.12

Open the Event Editor, which should currently be empty as shown in Figure 14.13. Next, double-click New condition to open the New Condition dialog box (Figure 14.14). Double-click the object that looks like a keyboard and mouse to display a menu like Figure 14.15. Choose The Keyboard > Upon Pressing a Key from the menu to display a dialog box like Figure 14.16. Press the up arrow key on your keyboard to create the event.

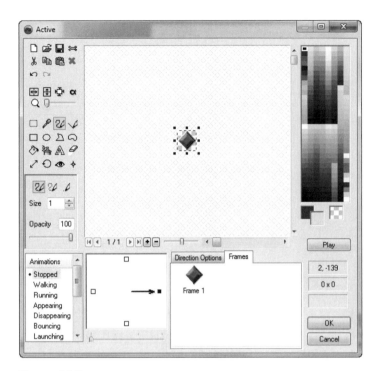

Figure 14.6
Selecting the entire image.

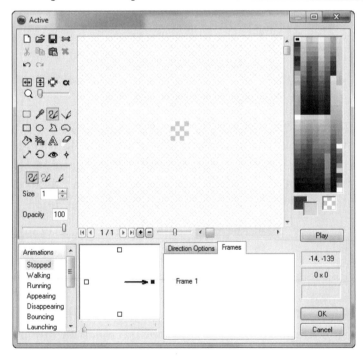

Figure 14.7
Erasing the image quickly.

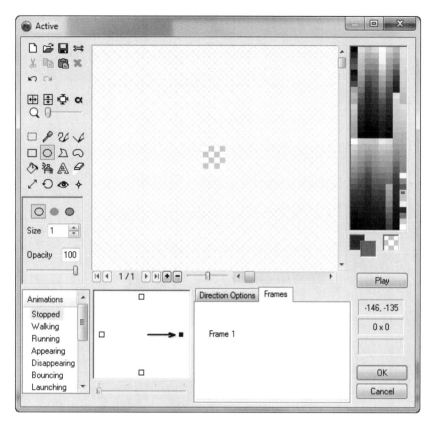

Figure 14.8
The Ellipse tool.

Figure 14.9
Choose a shade of red.

Figure 14.10
Pick the shaded option to draw the circle.

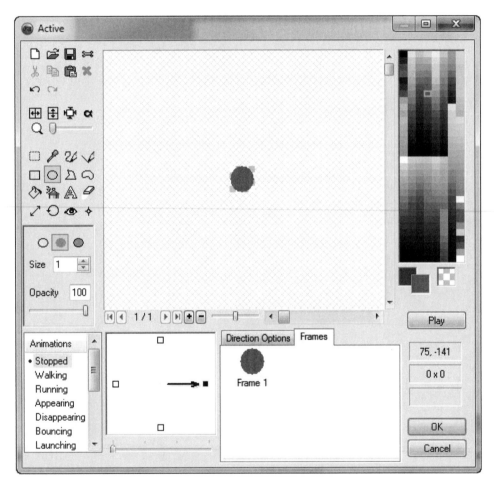

Figure 14.11
The drawn circle.

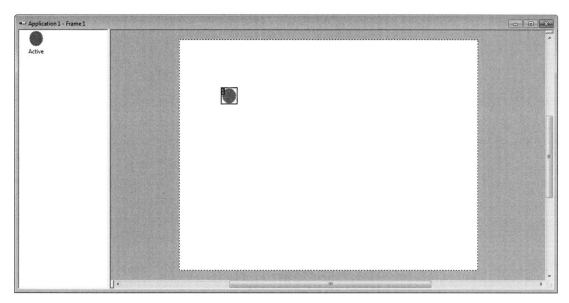

Figure 14.12
The circle in the Frame Editor.

Figure 14.13
The empty Event Editor.

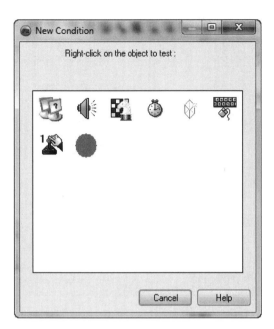

Figure 14.14
New Condition dialog box.

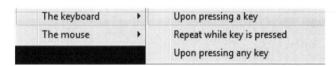

Figure 14.15
Keyboard and mouse events.

Figure 14.16
Choose a key.

Your Event Editor should now look like Figure 14.17. Right-click the box beneath the circle and in the same row as the event you created. From the menu that appears (Figure 14.18), choose Scale/Angle > Set X Scale to open the Enter Scale dialog box (Figure 14.19). Click the Retrieve Date from Current Object button to open the New Expression window (Figure 14.20). Right-click the Circle Active object to display a menu (Figure 14.21), and from the menu, select Scale/Angle > Get X Scale. This will give

Figure 14.17
The Event Editor.

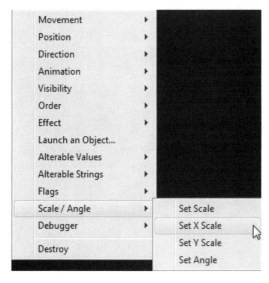

Figure 14.18
Scale and angle options.

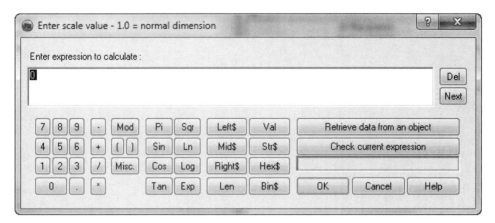

Figure 14.19
Enter Scale Value dialog box.

Figure 14.20
New Expression window.

you the current X Scale of the object. We are pressing the up arrow, so let's simply add a 1 to this (Figure 14.22). Another window will appear when you click OK (Figure 14.23). You can leave as is. Repeat the previous steps using the Y Scale for the object.

Once you are finished with the Y scale, you should see an event like the one displayed in Figure 14.24.

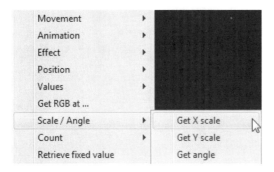

Figure 14.21
The menu displayed.

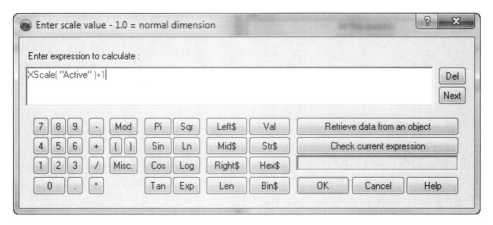

Figure 14.22
Adding 1 to the object.

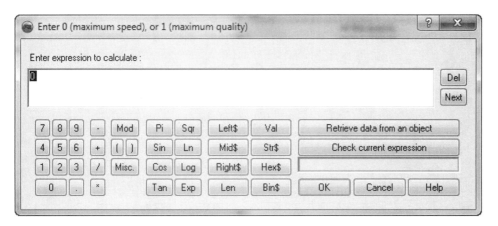

Figure 14.23
Leave as is.

Figure 14.24
The Y scale added too.

If you run the frame, and then click the up arrow, you will see the object resize. You can go back and add the down arrow options and subtract 1 from the object X scale and Y scale. Your Event Editor should look like Figure 14.25.

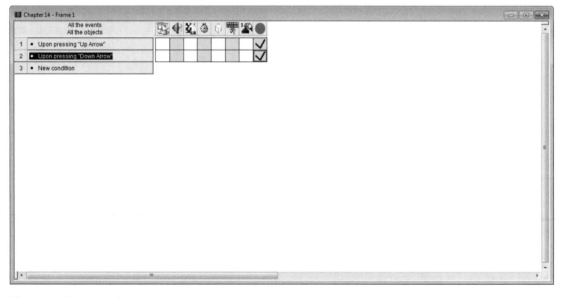

Figure 14.25
Subtracting now added.

If you run the scene now, you can quickly press the up arrow and down arrow so that you can see how this would allow you to simulate 3D in your application. Figures 14.26 to Figure 14.41 show the object getting larger and smaller as we press the up and down arrows.

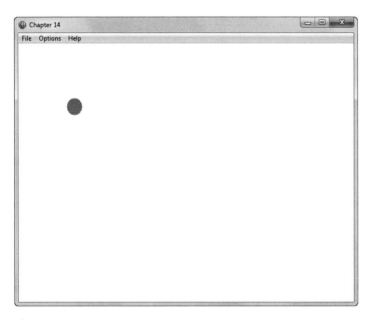

Figure 14.26

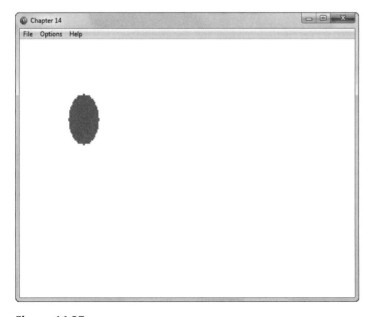

Figure 14.27

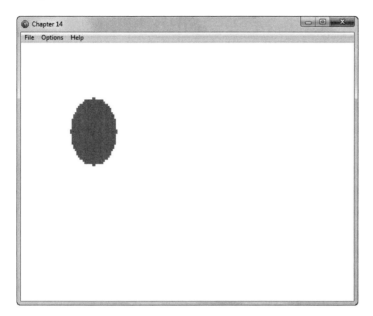

Figure 14.28

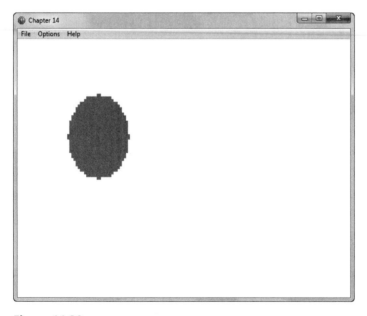

Figure 14.29

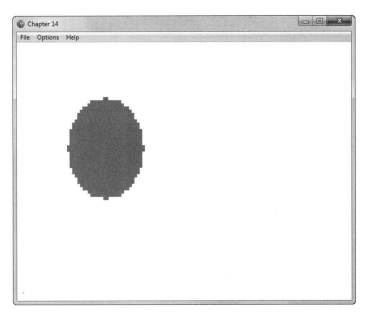

Figure 14.30

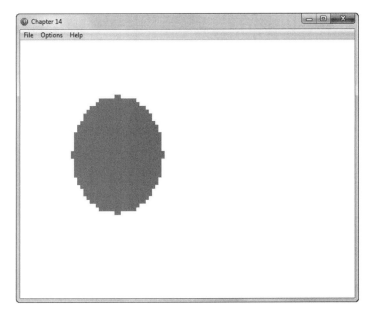

Figure 14.31

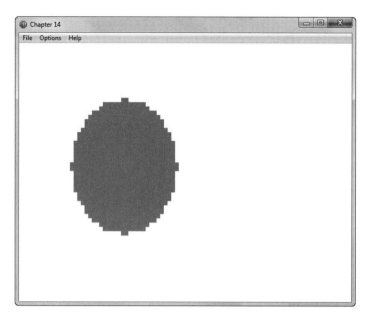

Figure 14.32

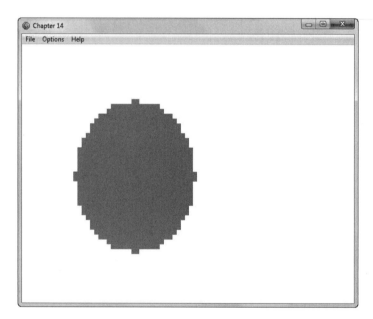

Figure 14.33

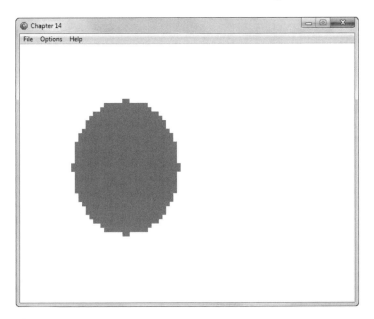

Figure 14.34

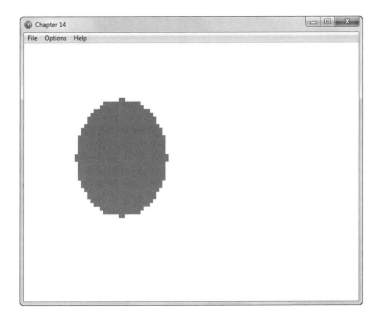

Figure 14.35

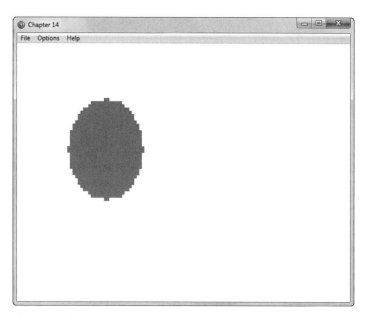

Figure 14.36

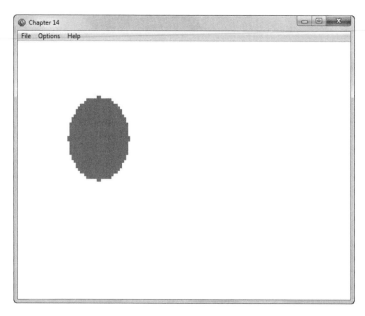

Figure 14.37

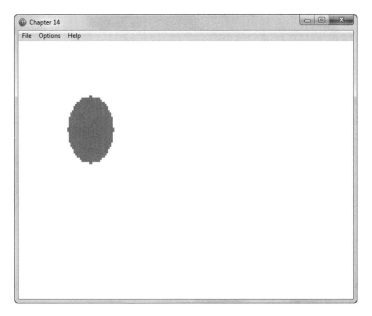

Figure 14.38

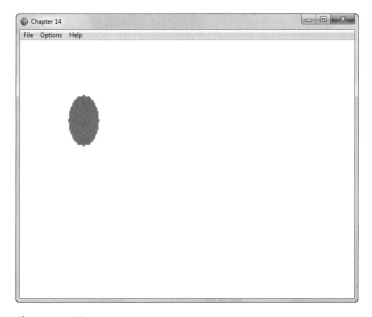

Figure 14.39

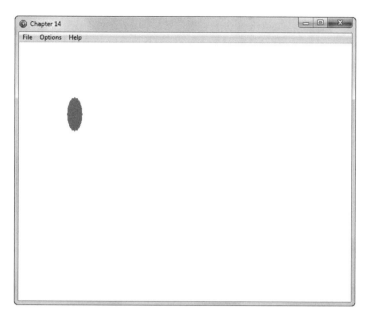

Figure 14.40

Figure 14.41

You can now see how you could use scaling to achieve a simulated 3D environment with just a couple of events. You could replace the circle object with something more realistic, like an asteroid, and by setting up a timer, you could simulate the object moving automatically toward your first-person view. This is just one example of how you could use this simulation for your games. If you execute the button presses quickly, it would appear as though the circle was moving toward or away from the player's perspective. We can even add to this by including things such as mock shadows and movement in the X and Y 2D coordinates. You could also use an Active Picture object for more precise resizing options.

CHAPTER REVIEW

In this chapter, we looked at 3D options we have at our disposal to simulate 3D in MMF. In the next chapter, we'll look at how to handle a deck of cards in your iOS and PC games you create inside MMF.

CHAPTER 15

DECK OF CARDS IN MMF

In Chapter 14, we learned how to simulate 3D in our games. In this chapter, we'll change directions to learn how we can simulate a deck of cards in MMF.

DRAWING A DECK OF CARDS

Drawing a deck of cards for a game can take some time, but it's not too difficult. We'll draw a simple card in GIMP so that you can see how easy it actually is.

Four-suit playing cards are usually made up of four distinct shapes: hearts, spades, clubs, and diamonds. These four shapes are generally universal and serve to identify the type of cards in a standard 52-card game deck.

While you could manually draw the shapes, and it wouldn't be difficult, there is a much easier way. Many people are already familiar with the shortcut keys that can allow you to enter these and many other shapes into your applications. These shapes are accessible from your keyboard using the ALT + number series combination. Unfortunately, these hotkeys don't work the same for graphic editors such as the GIMP. The GIMP uses CTRL+SHIFT+U followed by the Unicode for the corresponding symbol.

Open the GIMP and create a new image 70 × 100 pixels (Figure 15.1) by selecting File > New from the menu. Your image will be displayed and will look like Figure 15.2.

We are going to add text to the drawing, and it's important to remember that the color of the text will depend on the foreground color, which you can set by double-clicking the foreground color (Figure 15.3) in the Toolbox. This will open

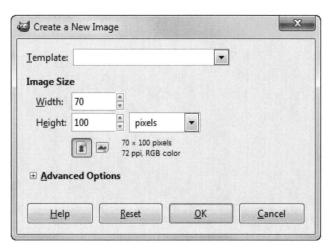

Figure 15.1
Create a new image.

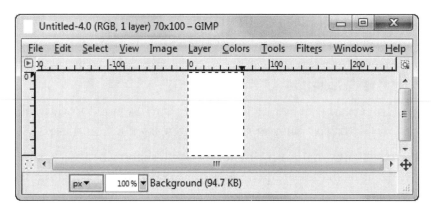

Figure 15.2
Your new image.

Figure 15.3
Foreground color.

the Change Foreground Color dialog box (Figure 15.4). Once you've selected the color you want, click OK. For playing cards, red colors are for diamonds and hearts, whereas black is for spades and clubs.

Click the Text tool in the Toolbox dialog or click Tools > Text in the menu. This will open the GIMP Text Editor dialog (Figure 15.5) in which you can enter your

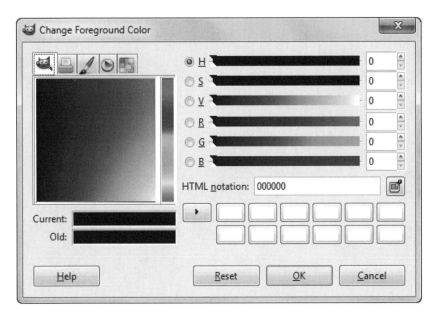

Figure 15.4
Selecting the foreground color.

Figure 15.5
Gimp Text Editor.

symbols. The symbol values are as follows:

u2660: spades

u2663: clubs

u2665: hearts

u2666: diamonds

Inside the Text dialog, create a solid spade by pressing CTRL+SHIFT+U and then typing 2660. In the Text dialog, it will look like an underlined "u2660" (Figure 15.6) until you press the Enter key. At that time, it will change into a solid spade symbol (Figure 15.7). You can create the other symbols using the Unicodes, but at this time, we'll concentrate on creating an Ace of Spades card. Click the Close button (Figure 15.8).

Figure 15.6
The "u2660" text.

Figure 15.7
The text changed into a shape.

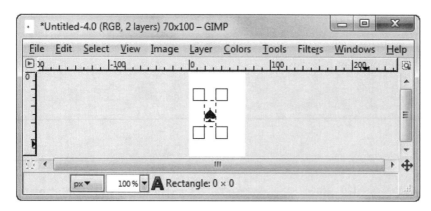

Figure 15.8
The card at this time.

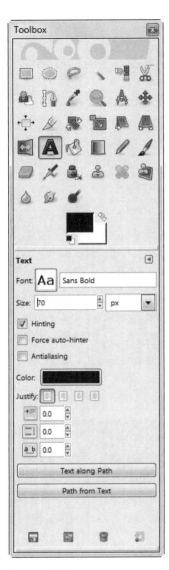

Figure 15.9
Changing the text size using the Toolbox's Text options.

With the text still selected, you can change the size of the symbol by clicking on the Text Size in the Toolbox, as seen in Figure 15.9. You can see the size changing as you move the options arrow up or down. When you have made it large enough for the middle of the card, you can create another symbol in the upper-left corner of the card, but in a much smaller size (Figure 15.10). Create a third shape and place in the bottom-right corner (Figure 15.11).

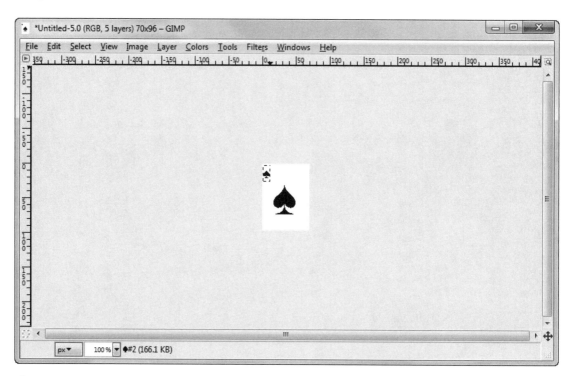

Figure 15.10
Creating the second symbol.

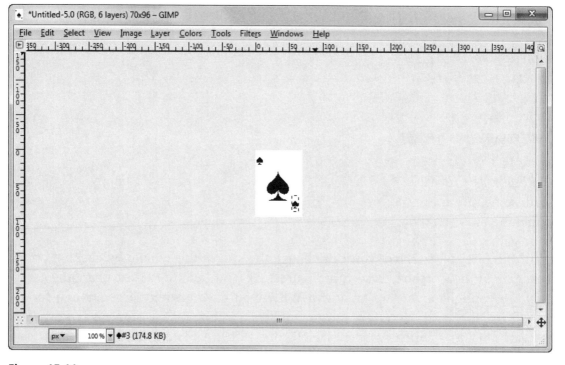

Figure 15.11
The final symbol for the card.

Figure 15.12
The Rotate tool.

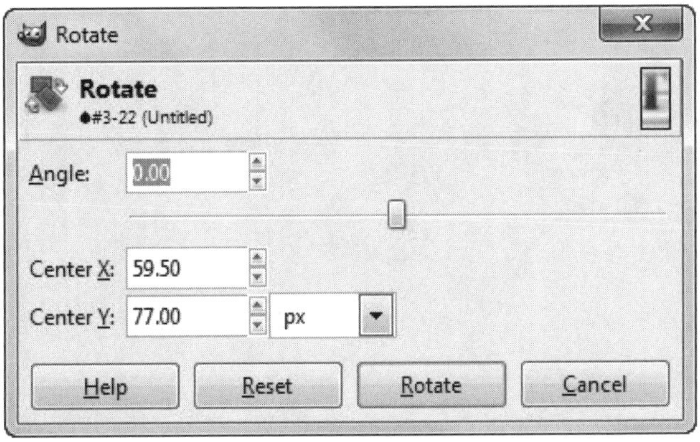

Figure 15.13
Rotate dialog box.

Click the Rotate tool (Figure 15.12). Once selected, click on the shape in the lower right to display the Rotate dialog box (Figure 15.13). From the dialog box that appears, choose 180 degrees and click Rotate. Your symbol will now be rotated as shown in Figure 15.14. To finish up your first card, you can add a regular letter A above the upper-left symbol, and another letter A below the bottom-right symbol. You can also rotate the second A to match the position of the symbol. The final card is shown in Figure 15.15.

It wouldn't be too difficult to create an entire deck of cards, but if you wish to download some pre-made images, you can check the following sites. However, please remember to check the copyright licenses before you simply use these graphics in your games:

http://www.ironstarmedia.co.uk/2010/01/free-game-assets-08-playing-card-pack/

http://freeware.esoterica.free.fr/html/freecards.html#pl

http://www.thehouseofcards.com/cards/card-images.html

http://www.fontriver.com/font/playing_cards/

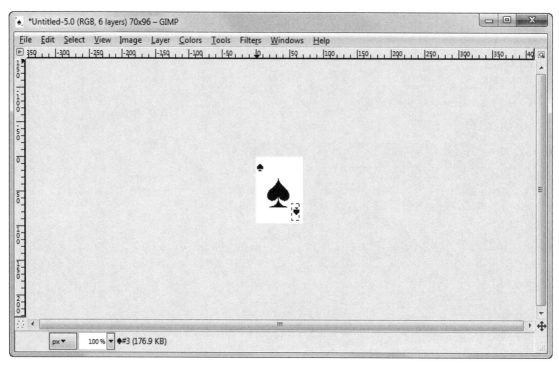

Figure 15.14
The symbol has been rotated.

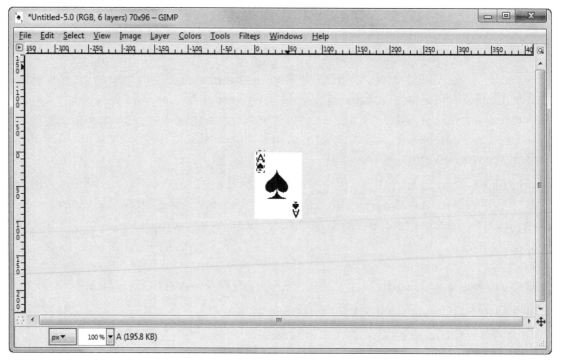

Figure 15.15
The final Ace of Spades card.

CARDS IN MMF

In a standard deck of cards, there are 52 separate cards. It's not too hard to represent the cards in MMF but before we move forward, you need to understand qualifiers and how they are used in MMF.

Qualifiers in MMF

A qualifier consists of a small icon and a name and can be applied to several related objects. For example, the "bad" qualifier can be applied to all of your enemies in a game, even if they are different objects. They all can have the "bad" qualifier. Under the Event Editor, the qualifier will appear in the list of objects. You can use the qualifier as you would any object. It simplifies programming the same event for all the baddies; instead of entering the action or condition for each of the bad guys, you simple use the "bad" qualifier and everything is done in one line.

The Qualifier dialog box is simple. Click on the Add button to choose from the list of available qualifiers. Select a qualifier and press Delete to remove it.

Now that you understand qualifiers, how will we plan to use them to represent a deck of cards? It's quite simple really. We need to create 52 separate active objects, which will represent all of our cards. Open MMF and create a new project (Figure 15.16).

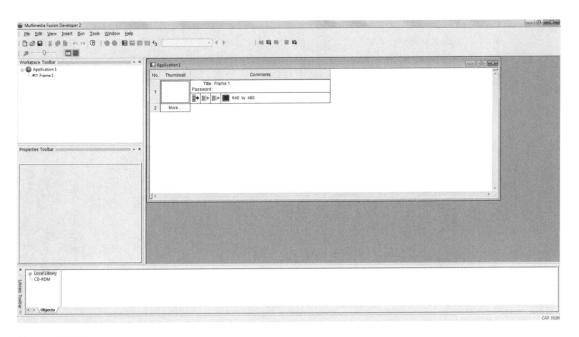

Figure 15.16
New application in MMF.

Next, let's add our first active object to the scene by opening the Frame Editor and selecting Insert > New Object to open the Create New Object window (Figure 15.17). Choose Active Object and click OK (Figure 15.18).

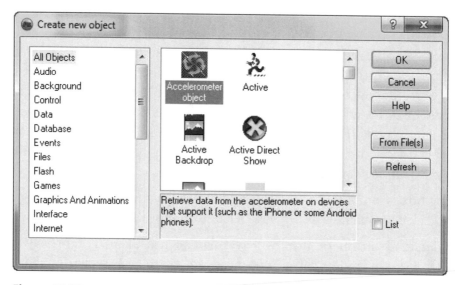

Figure 15.17
Create New Object window.

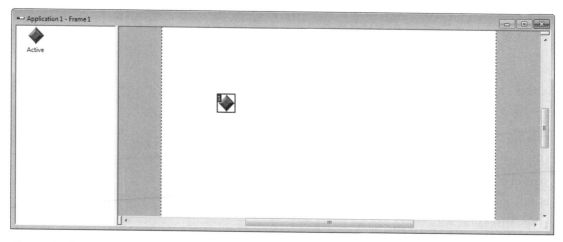

Figure 15.18
Active object in the Frame Editor.

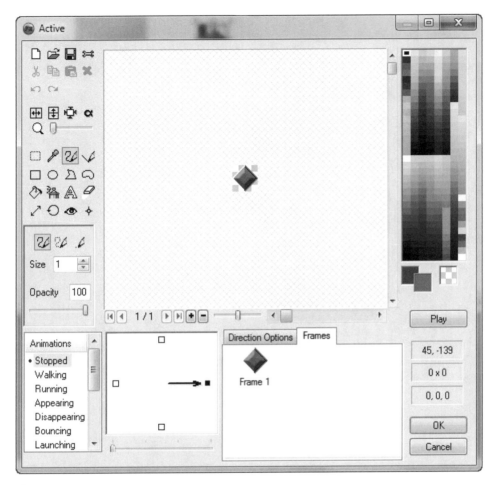

Figure 15.19
The Graphic Editor for the Active object.

Double-click the Active object diamond shape to open the Graphic Editor (Figure 15.19). Click the Open button in the upper left and then open the image you created of the card earlier (Figure 15.20). We need to make sure that our image is left alone as far as transparency goes, so in the Import Options dialog box double-click the color square left of the Pick button. This opens the Colors dialog box that looks like Figure 15.21. There, choose any color with the exception of black or white (Figure 15.22) and click OK. Click OK in the Import Options window and then click OK again. Your frame now looks like Figure 15.23.

Figure 15.20
Importing our card image.

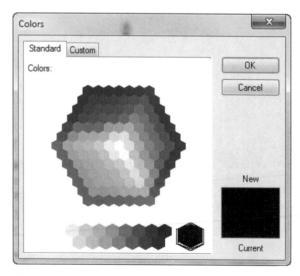

Figure 15.21
The Colors dialog box.

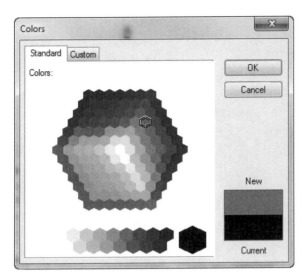

Figure 15.22
Choose any color.

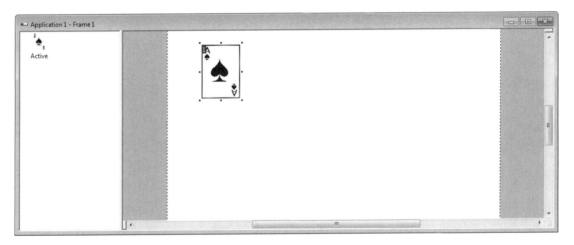

Figure 15.23
The frame with the card in it.

With the card selected, from the Properties window click the About tab, which is the right-most icon tab (Figure 15.24). Change the name to 1spades (Figure 15.25). You can also edit the icon if you wish by clicking the Icon line and then the Edit button. Open the same image for this using the Import option in the editor as you did for

Figure 15.24
The About tab.

Figure 15.25
Name your Active object 1spades.

Figure 15.26
The icon has changed.

Figure 15.27
Setting qualifiers for the cards.

importing the card. Click OK and you will now have an icon that better represents your image (Figure 15.26).

In the Properties window, click the Events tab, which is to the left of the About tab (Figure 15.27). This is where we will set the qualifiers for all of the cards. Click the

Figure 15.28
This will open the Edit button.

Figure 15.29
The Object Qualifiers window.

box to the right of Qualifiers and it will display an Edit button (Figure 15.28). Click the Edit button to display the Object Qualifiers window (Figure 15.29). Click the Add button (Figure 15.30). Click Good and then OK. Your window will now look life Figure 15.31. Click the OK button and you will see the qualifier listed in the

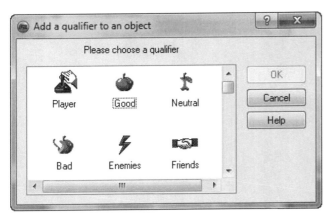

Figure 15.30
Choose the object that gets a qualifier.

Figure 15.31
The Good qualifier.

Properties window (Figure 15.32). That's all there is to setting the qualifier. You need to repeat this same setup for the remaining 51 cards, making sure to set the Qualifier to Good for each. You can see all of the cards added in Figure 15.33 and placed outside of the viewable frame. We'll place the cards in the viewable area when needed.

Figure 15.32
You can see qualifiers in the window.

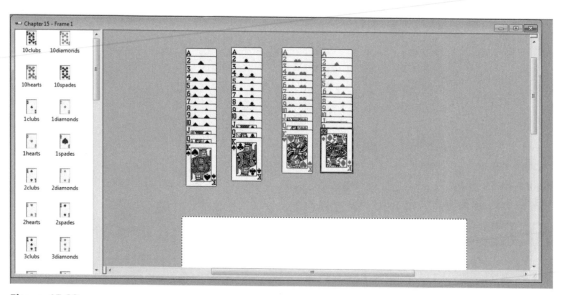

Figure 15.33
The cards are placed above the viewable area.

We'll use the Random Pool object to shuffle and organize our cards. You can add it by clicking Insert > New Object and clicking on it (Figure 15.34). When you add it, you will be presented with the Random Pool default options window (Figure 15.35). You can set the values as seen in Figure 15.36 and then click OK.

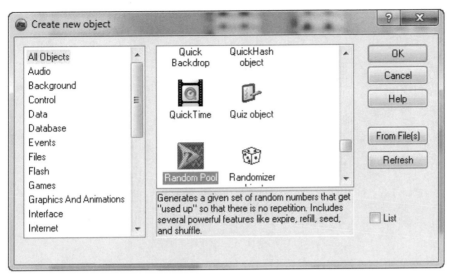

Figure 15.34
The New Object window.

Figure 15.35
The Random Pool window.

Figure 15.36
Set the options using this example.

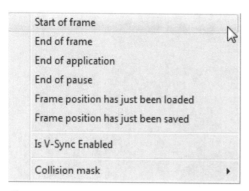

Figure 15.37
Select Start of Frame.

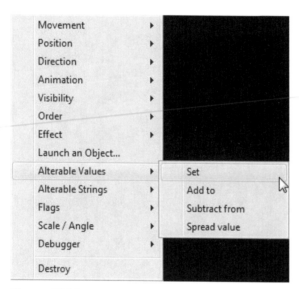

Figure 15.38
Drop-down menu.

There are 13 cards each of spades, diamonds, clubs, and hearts. We now need to set up some variables to track them. Open the Event Editor and select New Condition (Figure 15.37). Choose Start of Frame from the menu. Right-click the box beneath the first card in the list in the Start of Frame event (Figure 15.38). Choose a value of 1, and then click OK. Repeat this for the other cards in order from 2 to 52.

Open the Frame Editor and create a New Button (Figure 15.39) by selecting Insert > New Object. Once the button is placed, we need to change some settings by clicking Settings in the Properties window (Figure 15.40). Change the Text field to read "New Card" (Figure 15.41).

Open the Event Editor and select New Condition (Figure 15.42). We need to choose the button we added and then choose "Button clicked?" (Figure 15.43). Now, we need

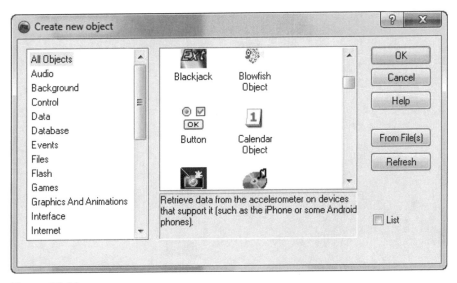

Figure 15.39
Create a new button in frame.

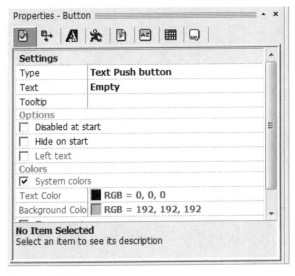

Figure 15.40
The button's properties.

Figure 15.41
Changing the text on the button.

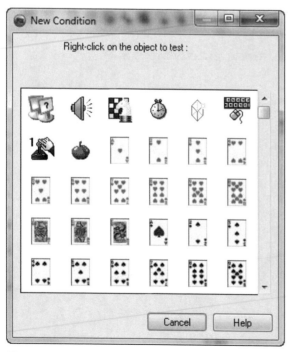

Figure 15.42
The Event Editor.

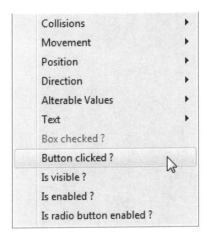

Figure 15.43
The drop-down menu with options.

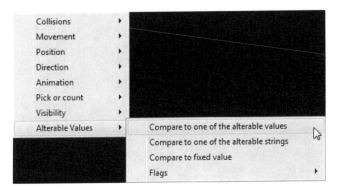

Figure 15.44
These menu options are displayed.

to set a couple of options for the Random Pool. In the first event, right-click the box to its right in the Random Pool column. From the options menu, choose Shuffle. This shuffles the cards at the start of the frame. Next, right-click the square to the right of the Button clicked? event (event 2) in the Random Pool column. From the options menu, choose Generate Number.

Next, select the New Condition and from the window, double-click the Group.Good object. This will display a menu like Figure 15.44. From the menu, select Alterable Values > Compare to One of the Alterable Values, which displays a window like Figure 15.45. Click Retrieve Date from Object. Find the Random Pool object and right-click on it (Figure 15.46). Choose Get Number Generated from the window

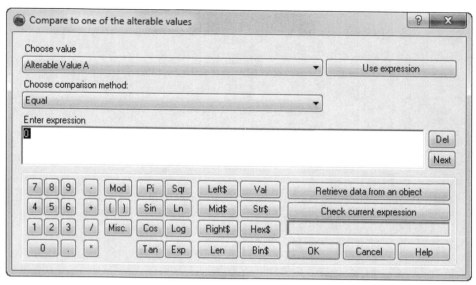

Figure 15.45
Compare to Value dialog.

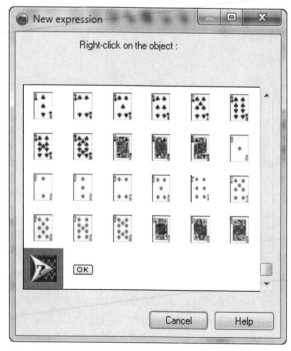

Figure 15.46
The New Expression window.

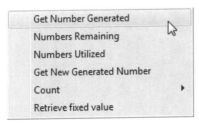

Figure 15.47
The drop-down menu is displayed when you right-click.

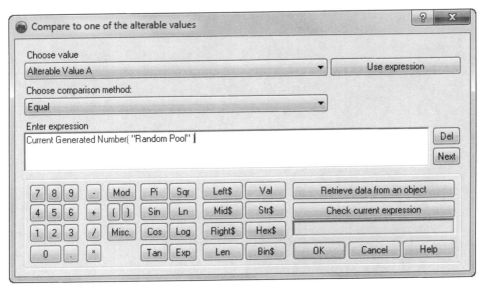

Figure 15.48
The expression has been created.

(Figure 15.47) and click OK (Figure 15.48). Click OK again. Your Event Editor should look like Figure 15.49.

Right-click the box beneath Group.Good and to the right of event 3, which will display a menu like Figure 15.50. Choose Position > Select Position and click an empty space approximating the position in Figure 15.51. It doesn't really matter where you place it but it needs to be in a visible location. The final step is to right-click the same square and choose Order > Bring to Front (Figure 15.52). You can now save your application and run it (Figure 15.53). Click the New Card

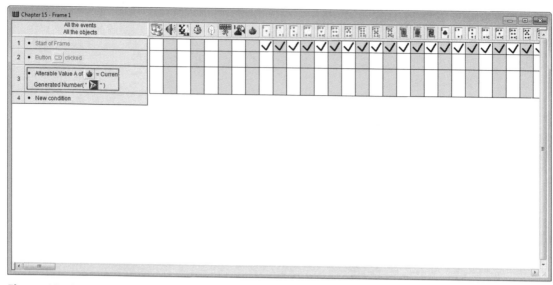

Figure 15.49
The Event Editor.

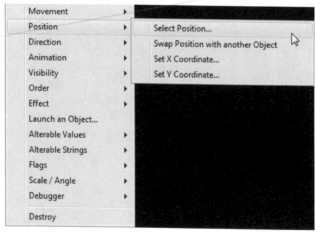

Figure 15.50
The drop-down menus.

button to test (Figure 15.54). You can continue trying New Card several times to make sure it changes (Figures 15.55 and 15.56).

With the Random Pool object, it's relatively easy to go through a deck of cards. You can use the values to determine the value of a hand and make a complete card game.

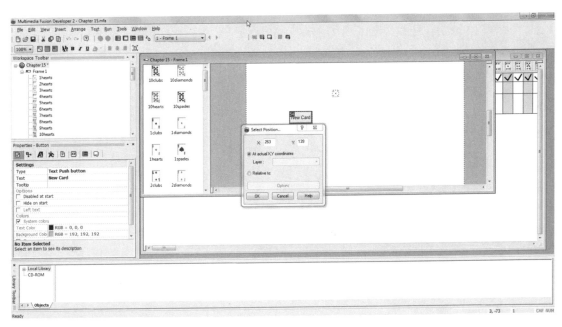

Figure 15.51
Set a location similar to this one.

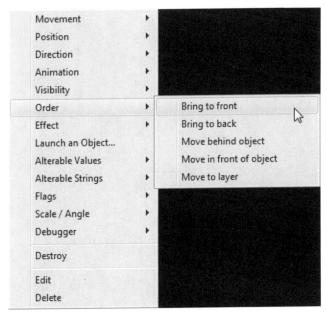

Figure 15.52
Setting the order of the cards to display on top.

Figure 15.53
The application is running.

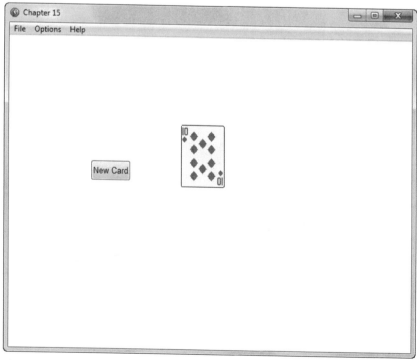

Figure 15.54
Testing the application.

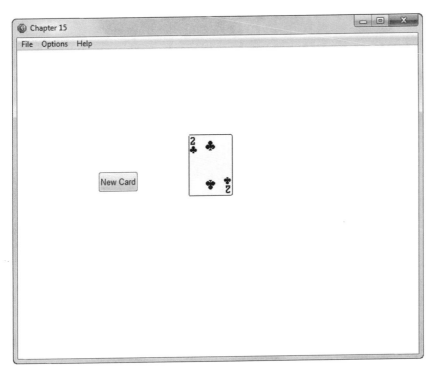

Figure 15.55
Testing the application.

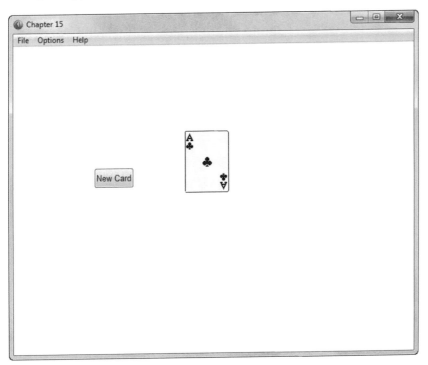

Figure 15.56
Testing the application.

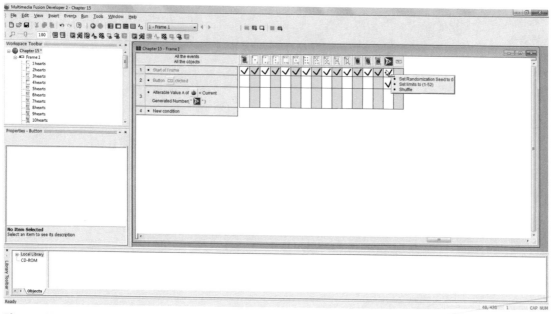

Figure 15.57
You might need to set these properties.

If you have an issue with the Random Pool object in which it doesn't want to move through to the next card, you can set the properties in the Event Editor using the Start of Frame event we created earlier. It does seem to occasionally have errors without it (Figure 15.57).

Chapter Review

In this chapter, we learned how to draw a set of cards in the GIMP and how to simulate a complete deck of 52 cards as the basis of future games in MMF.

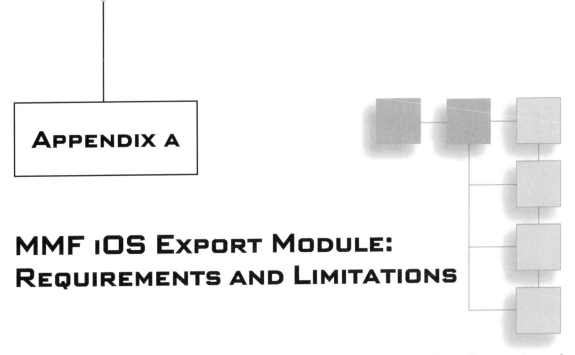

APPENDIX A

MMF iOS Export Module: Requirements and Limitations

There are some differences that you need to be aware of regarding the creation of iOS games in MMF, including a few related to memory, sound, graphics, interfaces, and the available extensions for iOS. A complete list is available below, but as extensions are added frequently by Clickteam and other developers, you can refer to www.clickteam.com for the ever-changing list.

Limitations/Differences with PC Runtime

There are a few differences related to graphics, sounds, fonts, and interface objects when you compare the iOS exporter with the PC version.

Graphics

The graphic engine of the MMF2 iOS runtime is hardware-accelerated, but it doesn't support shaders as well as the frame and layer effects of the HWA PC runtime. It supports the blending and RGB coefficients at the same time as standard effects.

Even if it's an hardware-accelerated runtime, graphic memory and processor power are limited compared with a Windows machine. Follow the rules described in the help file to limit the memory your application uses.

Sounds

The iOS runtime supports WAV and MP3 files. Sounds that are not in WAV or MP3 format are converted to WAV. Limitation: As there is a single hardware MP3 decoder you should avoid playing several MP3 files at the same time.

External Files

Very few objects support external files:

- Array
- INI
- Hi-score

They load/save files from/to the bundle of the application. You can include default files for the Array and INI objects (and the List object in the next update).

Strings and Fonts

PC fonts are replaced by their iOS equivalent when running on the device. PC and iOS fonts are not always the same size; you might have to enlarge the string objects so that the text is displayed properly.

Interface Objects

The iOS runtime has its own interface objects (button, single- and multiple-line edit box). Most of the standard interface objects are either not available or have limited features.

Specific iOS Objects

- Accelerometer
- iOS
- iOS Button
- iOS Multiple Line Edit Box
- iOS Single Line Edit Box
- iOS Store
- Joystick Control
- Multiple Touch
- Camera and GameCenter (MMF2 Developer only)

Supported Standard and Third-Party Extensions

- Active Object
- Active Backdrop

- Active System Box
- Advanced Direction
- Advanced Game Board
- Advanced Path Movement
- Array
- Backdrop
- Background System Box
- Button (limited features)
- Calculate Text Rect Object
- Clickteam Movement Controller
- Counter
- Date & Time
- Direction Calculator
- Easing
- Edit box (limited features)
- Get
- Hi-scores
- Immediate IF
- In And Out Controller
- INI
- Input
- Layer
- List box (limited features, no interface)
- Lives
- Location
- Move Safely 2
- Move It
- MT Random
- Object Mover

- Platform Movement
- Question and Answer
- Quick Backdrop
- Randomizer
- Score
- String
- String Parser
- String Tokenizer
- Sub-Application
- Wargame Map

Requirements and Limitations for Building MMF iOS Applications

Requirements for the iOS exporter:

- Registered version of MMF2 or MMF2 Developer on a Windows machine.
- A Macintosh computer running at least OS X Snow Leopard.
- You have to be registered as an iOS developer with Apple ($99 per year). Note: you can register a simple Developer account (free) and test your applications in the iPhone simulator, then register as an iOS developer later.
- Xcode and the latest version of iOS 4 SDK installed on the Mac.
- To test on a real device, you need an iPhone, iPod Touch, or iPad running iOS4.

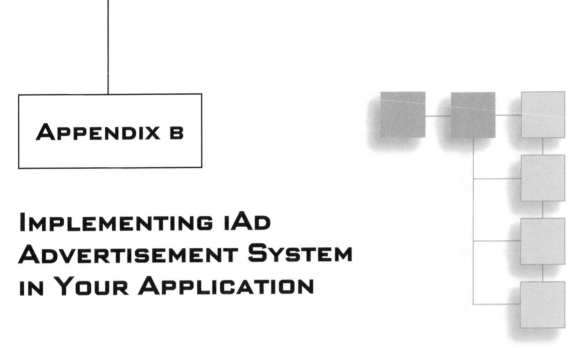

APPENDIX B

IMPLEMENTING iAd ADVERTISEMENT SYSTEM IN YOUR APPLICATION

Multimedia Fusion 2 Developer makes it really simple to incorporate iAd messages in your application. You just need to set a couple of properties. The system will initially display a fake advertisement for testing purposes. To allow real advertisements to be displayed, you must enroll in the Apple iAd program (for more information go to: http://advertising.apple.com/).

The iAd properties are located in the application's iOS property panel, and in the frame's iOS property panel.

APPLICATION PROPERTIES

- Enable iAd.
- Check this property to enable the iAd system in your application.
- Display ad on bottom of the screen. If unchecked, the ad will be displayed on the top of the screen. If checked, the ad will be displayed on the bottom.
- Frame property.
- Display Ad. Check this property to allow the ad to be displayed on the frame. If the property is unchecked, and an ad was displayed from a previous frame, it will disappear. This property allows you to decide which one of the frames of your application will contain adverts.
- Ad dimensions. A portrait-oriented iAd banner is 320 pixel wide and 50 pixels high. A landscape-oriented ad is 480 pixels wide and 32 pixels high. Wherever

you choose the ad to be, top or bottom, the ad will cover the application. You must design the application so that no important data is supposed to display at the location of the banner. If your application uses the touch joystick as a means of control, then you have no choice; you must put the banner on the top of the screen (we could have displayed the joystick higher, but we realized that it was very easy to make a mistake and touch the ad instead of the joystick, thus interrupting the game).

Note

The advertisement banner is only displayed when the application can connect to the ad server. If the ad cannot connect, it will simply disappear from the screen or not be initially displayed. Your application must cope with it, and be ready to run with the extra space on the display. Do not be surprised, if in a middle of an ad, the banner disappears; this means that the connection is lost. When you test your application under XCode, a fake advert is displayed. To allow complete testing of the system, Apple sometimes simulates an interruption of the connection to the server; the fake ad can disappear, as a true ad would do. In addition, you might run your application at the precise moment when the connection pretends to be interrupted. In this case, no ad will be displayed at the start of the application, but it will appear after a moment.

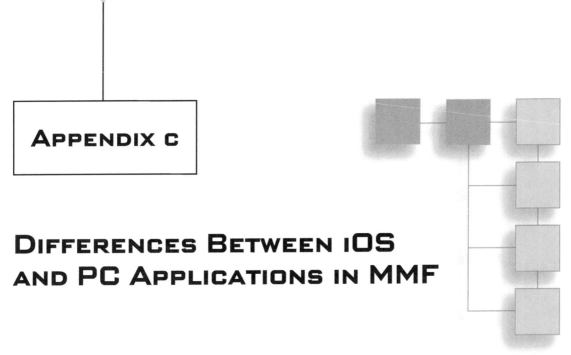

APPENDIX C

DIFFERENCES BETWEEN iOS AND PC APPLICATIONS IN MMF

MMF games are created with most of the same methods regardless of the platform you are developing for. That is, an iOS game is created basically the same as a game for the PC. However, there are slightly different options depending on your projects intended platform.

SOUNDS

Multimedia Fusion 2 Developer offers you two ways of playing sounds. The first one, called "AudioPlayer," is suitable for long sounds, like background music. Its main advantage is that it does not store the entire sound in memory prior to playing, thus taking up less space. Its disadvantage is that it takes some processing power when the sound is started, slowing down the application. This time-lag makes it a bad choice for playing in-game sounds.

The second way to play sound is to use OpenAL. It is suitable for short sounds. It does need the sound to be stored in memory prior to playing, but it does not take any processing power when the sound starts. OpenAL is a good choice for short sounds in the middle of the game. When you use a "Play sample" action in iOS mode, you have a new check box at your disposal, named "Play with AudioPlayer." This check box has three states:

- **Unchecked.** The sound will be played using OpenAL
- **Checked.** The sound will be played using AudioPlayer

- **Undetermined.** Multimedia Fusion 2 Developer looks at the duration of the sound. If it is fewer than 15 seconds, then it is played with OpenAL; if it is more than 15 seconds, it is played with AudioLayer. This is the automatic mode.

The default setting is automatic mode. Basically, you should check the box only for background music, or leave it undetermined.

Please note that the Set Sample Position action works with AudioPlayer, but not with OpenAL (except for position 0), and that the Set Sample Frequency action works only with OpenAL.

MP3: iOS Supports MP3 Sounds

The iPhone exporter for Multimedia Fusion 2 Developer adds an MP3 filter, to allow you to insert MP3 sounds into your applications. Be careful though, iPhones/iPads/iPods have a single MP3 hardware decoder, so you should use MP3 sounds only for background music. And do not play several MP3 sounds at the same time. You can also use the new MP3 filter to play MP3 sounds in your Windows applications; however, this filter just calls the decoding API of Windows, so it depends on codecs already installed on the end user's machine (Windows usually ships with an MP3 codec though). Note: if you redistribute an application that contains MP3 sounds, you may need to get an MP3 license (at the date this documentation was written, a license was not required for any entity with an MP3-related gross revenue less than $100,000, but the terms of this license may change; check them from time to time on mp3licensing.com).

Edit Object

The iOS runtime supports the Edit object, but you must be aware that only a few properties of the object are supported under iOS:

- Multiple-lines
- Border, only for single-line objects
- Editable, only for single-line objects
- Vertical scroll-bar, only for multiple-line objects
- Text and background color

Object Font

The object also uses the standard iOS keyboards, and is automatically positioned in the center of the screen above the keyboard when editing. If you want a finer control on the object, just use the iOS Single Line Edit object, or the iOS Multiple Lines Edit object.

RUNNING THE APPLICATION ON VARIOUS SERVICES

Multimedia Fusion 2 Developer does its best to allow your application to run on various screen sizes. The window size of the application is smaller than the device screen size. The application is zoomed and centered in the display. You do not need to bother with anything, the process is completely transparent to you (screen and touch coordinates are zoomed, etc.). For example, it is perfectly possible to run a 320 × 480 application on an iPad.

The Window Size of the Application Is Bigger Than the Device Screen Size

The application is reduced and centered on the device screen. Here, too, the process is completely transparent to you. It is perfectly possible to run an iPad application (768 × 1024) on a 3rd-Gen iPhone (320 × 480).

The Application Is the Same Size as the Device Screen

The application is displayed without zoom. The auto-zooming feature of Multimedia Fusion 2 Developer allows you to create applications in the best possible resolution without having to bother about which device it will run on. We suggest that, for an iPhone application, you choose a window size of 640 × 960; it will appear high-resolution on a 4th-Gen iPhone and will work fine on a 3rd- and 2nd-Gen iPhone.

FONTS

PC fonts are replaced by their iOS equivalent when running on the device. Things to know:

- Some of the fonts do not contain italic or bold, or both at the same time.
- The Helvetica font is mapped to the system font on iOS (which is a Helvetica font by the way). So if you prefer to use the system font, choose Helvetica on the PC. The system font can be bold or italic but not at the same time.
- If a font does not exist on iOS, it's replaced by the system font.

STRING OBJECTS

The fonts on iOS do not have exactly the same size as their PC equivalent. You might have to enlarge the string objects so that the text displays properly.

OLD DEVICE LIMITATIONS WITH THE HWA EXPORTER

3G and 2G iPhones and iPods (3GS and up aren't affected) have some limitations when it comes to the HWA blending modes. Blending coefficients are applied *after* the Ink effect is applied. This means that using the "invert" Ink effect does not give the same results.

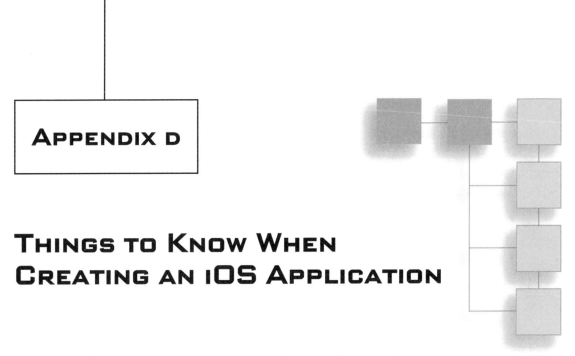

APPENDIX D

THINGS TO KNOW WHEN CREATING AN iOS APPLICATION

This appendix contains some important things to know when you create an application for the iPhone or the iPad. Please read it carefully and keep it in mind when programming your application.

BUILDING FOR VARIOUS DEVICES

Multimedia Fusion 2 Developer allows you to build applications that can run on an iPhone, iPod Touch, or iPad. As a default, the properties of the XCode project are set to iPhone/iPad, meaning that your application will work on any of the available Apple devices at that date.

If you want to restrict your application to iPod only, in XCode, right-click on the name of your project in the project window (top most item) and choose "Get info." This will display the properties of the project. Scroll down a few pages until you find the line called "Targeted Device Family." Select iPod in the combo box. If you want your application to only work on an iPad, select iPad in the combo box.

MEMORY CONSIDERATIONS

iOS devices are portable devices. As such, the amount of useable memory (RAM, not to be confused with the amount of Flash memory where the files are stored) is limited. On a 2nd-Gen device, like the original iPhone and the 2nd-Gen iPod, the size of RAM is 128 MB. On 3rd-Gen devices and over, the amount of RAM is 256 MB.

This might seem a lot, but if you know that iOS 4 consumes at least 80 MB to function, you quickly realize that the amount of working memory on a 2nd-Gen device can be evaluated to around 40 MB.

The code of an iOS application must be copied into RAM before being launched by iOS: this takes 2 MB out of your previous RAM. The conclusion is that, if you want your application to work on a 2nd-Gen device, you have to be very careful about the size of your graphics and sounds. The next section will give you tips to reduce the memory imprint of your graphics.

If your game cannot run on such a device, then you should prevent it from being distributed in the App Store for a 2nd-Gen device. If you do so, you will save some memory by setting the build architecture of the application in the project properties to Arm7 only, avoiding the duplication of the compiled code.

HOW TO FIND OUT EXACTLY HOW MUCH MEMORY YOUR APPLICATION TAKES

The amount of memory used by an application is shown in the debugger window (top-left of the screen) when you launch your application in Multimedia Fusion 2 Developer. The memory displayed is evaluated for a PC application, and does not reflect the amount of RAM really taken by your application under iOS. To find out exactly how much memory your application needs on the device, in XCode, launch your application by choosing the menu option "Run/Run with performance tools/Allocations." XCode will automatically open a window that keeps real-time track of all the memory allocations of your application. You will find the total amount of RAM used in the first line of the grid.

Be sure to check every frame of your application, as the amount of memory used depends on the amount of graphics and sounds used in each frame. Also check that the number of allocations (not the temporary allocations, which keep growing normally) does not increase as your game runs (and might indicate undestroyed objects).

Save Memory for Graphics

Alpha-Channels

Alpha-channels look awesome and give a visually pleasing effect, but they will slow down your game if you overuse them, just as they do in the PC runtime (just more).

An image with an alpha-channel takes 33% more memory and space than an image without, and it takes more power and time to render them.

Workaround   Does your graphic really need the alpha-channel? Does the background underneath it ever change? If not you could probably "bake" the alpha-channel effect into the image itself so that the shadow is just part of the picture.

Huge Pictures

Many are often tempted to import really large pictures into the game where it will only show very little of that picture at one time. It's better to break it up into smaller parts so that fewer of them are shown at one time. Remember that any image you have in your game has to fit inside its own texture.

In a sample game there was a 960 × 480 background image on a frame. This picture alone had to fit into a 1024 × 512 texture taking up a huge amount of memory. What was even worse was that it had an alpha-channel even though no pixel in it was transparent. Second, the same frame had two different huge animations sized 957 × 158 (each of them contained 17 frames). This already takes up 2*17 * 1024*256 * 3 = 26738688 bytes = 25.5 MB of RAM, which is way above what the iOS likes. That was even without the rest of the graphics and the huge background image we talked about before.

Workaround   Most graphics don't need 100% crispness and quality. It will only take ¼th of the previous memory usage if you cut your image size in half and then at run-time scale it to 2.0. It will also run much faster as it utilizes the graphics card RAM cache much better.

Crop your images to remove any useless empty space around them. Some developers tend to use a single frame size for an entire animation with huge transparent parts in some images. It's probably better at design time, but at runtime it results in a loss of time and space.

Try to make your graphics of a size close to something of a power of two. It will waste less precious memory.

A power-of-two size is one of the following: 8, 16, 32, 64, 128, 256, 512, 1024. Images less than 8 × 8 pixels will be stored in an 8 × 8 texture as they cannot be smaller than that. You can easily use different sizes for your width and height; they don't have to be equal.

Be sure to set the "Image compression" property to "Color reduction" either globally for all objects in the App iOS properties or per object—as often as you can. In many cases it will make it consume half the memory it did before. Take, for example, the big background image we mentioned before: it wasted 2 MB of texture memory. With color compression and no alpha-channel, it will only require 1 MB. And if it was cropped to only fill out the resolution of the iPhone device, it would only require 30 KB. The animations mentioned before that took 25 MB of RAM, can with color compression and half the resolution only take: $2*17 * 512*128 * 2 = 4456448$ bytes = 4.25 MB! That is a huge difference.

Single-Color Graphic

This is kind of an extension to the previous pitfall: As a suggestion from Clickteam, the makers of MMF see some big active objects (typical white) that are meant to cover the entire screen and fade to transparent that are still stored in memory uncompressed at runtime and waste just as much memory as if it were a pretty picture.

Workaround If you need those fade effects, you can again scale a small active to fit the screen at runtime and gradually alter its semi-transparency. You should, in general, avoid using transitions on objects larger than the device screen resolution even though it works well enough. Using a transition on such an object will consume a lot of extra memory during the transition and can be slow.

You have to try it at runtime to see if it gives you a noticeable performance drop. Just remember that even though it doesn't hurt the FPS that much, it can still drain the battery much more than you know.

Speed Considerations

Though it may not be as big of a performance issue, overuse of "text" counters/score and strings can hurt your game's performance a little bit. If the text doesn't change, it should not be a performance problem, but if you update your string/score/counters often (as counters/scores often do) you will get a performance problem.

Workaround Only use text whenever you know it will not change often (like every frame). Use bitmap counters/scores instead of text counters/scores. There you can also control the visual style of your objects and there is no performance penalty.

Too Many Transitions at One Time

Each object that needs to have a transition effect on it will consume more memory than usual and will use some special buffers on the device that aren't unlimited. Once you reach a certain limit you will begin getting errors. Also, if you have many transitions going on at one time it will slow down performance.

Workaround Instead of using transitions, try using animations or other effects to give the same effect. Instead of using the "Fade" transition, manually setting the semi-transparency of your objects will be much faster and will not consume any more memory.

Unnecessary Ink Effects

We have seen other games almost ready for release where INK effects are unnecessarily used too often. Having a big background covering the screen and setting it to either transparent or ADD so that it will be added to some gradient behind it will only make your game slower and consume more power. Instead, create your graphics as they should look at runtime and then use them like that.

Workaround Ink effects are only meant for places where you cannot modify the original image to look like it should at edit time. For example, if you want a grayscale background from a picture, you make it grayscale before you import it into MMF2. You simply don't put the monochrome Ink effect on it and forget about it.

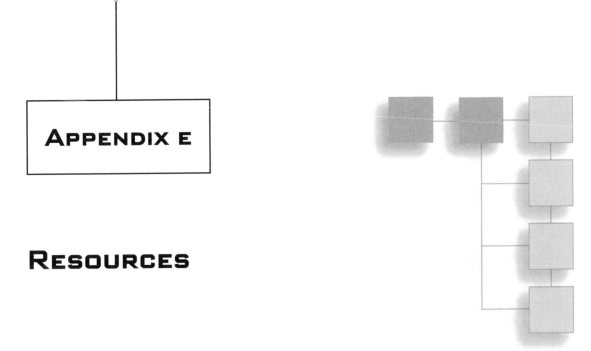

Appendix E

Resources

This appendix contains some links to royalty-free graphics, some of which are open-source or free graphics, some commercial graphics, and some royalty-free and commercial music and sound effects. A commercial license usually implies that you'll need to pay for the use of materials and may include very specific details on how you can use them. Open-source graphics have licenses too but are usually much less restrictive and freely available. As always, be sure to check current licenses before you assume you can use these in a commercial project.

2D Royalty-Free Graphics

http://opengameart.org/

http://www.lostgarden.com/search/label/free%20game%20graphics

http://www.lostgarden.com/2007/12/how-to-bootstrap-your-indie-art-needs.html

http://www.derekyu.com/tigs/assemblee/

http://pousse.rapiere.free.fr/tome/

http://bagfullofwrong.co.uk/bagfullofwords/abuse-my-ip-make-games/

http://www.dumbmanex.com/bynd_freestuff.html

3D Models
Commercial and Free Models

http://www.turbosquid.com/

http://www.the3dstudio.com/

http://www.frogames.net/content-packs.html

http://3docean.net/

http://www.polycount.com/forum/

http://www.thegnomonworkshop.com/

Free Textures

http://www.cgtextures.com/

http://www.mayang.com/textures/

Royalty-Free Music

http://www.newgrounds.com/audio/

http://sampleswap.org/

http://jewelbeat.com/free/

http://dig.ccmixter.org/

http://8bc.org/

http://incompetech.com/

http://www.jamendo.com/

http://modarchive.org/

http://www.indiegamemusic.com/

http://www.partnersinrhyme.com/pir/free_music_loops.shtml

http://musopen.com/

http://soundcloud.com/

http://bandcamp.com/

http://free-loops.com/free-loops.php

http://ocremix.org/

http://opsound.org/

http://www.publicdomain4u.com/

http://www.archive.org/details/netlabels

http://www.icompositions.com/music/

http://www.purple-planet.com/

http://www.archive.org/details/opensource_audio

http://phlow-magazine.com/

http://www.stonewashed.net/free-music.html

ROYALTY-FREE SOUNDS

http://www.soundsnap.com/

http://www.freesfx.co.uk/

http://www.stephanschutze.com/sound-library.html

http://www.epicsound.com/sfx/index.php

http://soundbible.com/

http://www.pacdv.com/sounds/index.html

http://www.partnersinrhyme.com/pir/PIRsfx.shtml

http://www.soundjay.com/

http://www.flashkit.com/soundfx/

http://www.derekyu.com/tigs/assemblee/

http://www.pdsounds.org/

COMMERCIAL MUSIC

http://www.soundrangers.com/

http://www.sounddogs.com/catsearch.asp?Type=2

http://www.jewelbeat.com/

http://luckylionstudios.com/

http://www.shockwave-sound.com/

http://www.audionetwork.com/production-music/

http://audiojungle.net/

http://www.premiumbeat.com/

http://www.sonycreativesoftware.com/loops

http://www.productiontrax.com/

http://www.partnersinrhyme.com/

http://www.soundloopstudio.com/

http://www.royaltyfreetunes.co.uk/

http://www.pond5.com/

http://www.audiomicro.com/

http://www.musicloops.com/

http://www.ibaudio.com/

http://www.audiosparx.com/sa/games_music/game_music.cfm

http://www.stockmusic.net/

Commercial Sounds

http://www.soundsnap.com/

http://www.soundrangers.com/

http://www.sounddogs.com/sound-effects.asp

http://www.shockwave-sound.com/

http://www.audionetworkplc.com/sound-effects/

http://www.sound-ideas.com/

http://www.sonycreativesoftware.com/content/soundeffects

http://audiojungle.net/

http://www.productiontrax.com/

http://www.pond5.com/

http://www.audiomicro.com/

http://www.1soundfx.com/

http://www.partnersinrhyme.com/

http://www.stockmusic.net/index.cfm/page/soundeffects.home

http://www.sound-effect.com/

INDEX